BrightRED Study Guide

Curriculum for Excellence

N5

ACCOUNTING

William Reynolds

BrightRED
PUBLISHING

First published in 2014. Reprinted with corrections in 2016 by:

Bright Red Publishing Ltd

1 Torphichen Street

Edinburgh

EH3 8HX

A CIP record for this book is available from the British Library.

ISBN 978-1-906736-52-1

With thanks to:
Partnership Publishing Solutions (layout), Clodagh Burke (copy-edit)
Cover design and series book design by Caleb Rutherford – e i d e t i c

Acknowledgements

Every effort has been made to seek all copyright holders. If any have been overlooked, then Bright Red Publishing will be delighted to make the necessary arrangements. Permission has been sought from all relevant copyright holders and Bright Red Publishing are grateful for the use of the following:

ailanlee/iStock.com (p 6); Beth (CC BY 2.0)[1] (p 6); hypnotype/Shutterstock.com (p 6); pipp/freeimages.com (p 8); Chris Potter/stockmoneys.com (CC BY 2.0)[1] (p 10); Images_ of_Money (CC BY 2.0)[1] (p 12); fotek/iStock.com (p 13); Adisa/Shutterstock.com (p 14); Ken Teegardin (CC BY-SA 2.0)[2] (p 16); Andrey_Popov/Shutterstock.com (p 19); Phil Wood (CC BY-ND 2.0)[3] (p 21); foxumon/freeimages.com (p 24); Minerva Studio/iStock.com (p 26); psphotograph/iStock.com (p 28); Deklofenak/Shutterstock.com (p 34); vichie81/ Shutterstock.com (p 37); monticelllo/iStock.com (p 37); Fantasista/iStock.com (p 38); Dave Dugdale (CC BY-SA 2.0)[2] (p 40); Eddi (CC BY 2.0)[1] (p 42); kirstypargeter/iStock.com (p 44); nkzs/freeimages.com (p 52); Stuart Miles/Shutterstock.com (p 54); Evan-Amos (public domain) (p 55); Caleb Rutherford (p 61); Andreas Steinbach/Dreamstime.com (p 61); mistermast/freeimages.com (p 61); elemental/freeimages.com (p 62); Commander, U.S. 7th Fleet (CC BY-SA 2.0)[2] (p 62); GordonBellPhotography/iStock.com (p66) Daemys/ Dreamstime.com (p 72); TaxRebate.org.uk (CC BY 2.0)[1] (p 74); joxxxxjo/iStock.com (p 76); Richard Peterson/Shutterstock.com (p 84); andresrimaging/iStock.com (p 90); cobrasoft/ freeimages.com (p 91); Sergey Skleznev/Dreamstime.com (p 93); IPGGutenbergUKLtd/ iStock.com (p 94).

(CC BY 2.0)[1]   http://creativecommons.org/licenses/by/2.0/
(CC BY-SA 2.0)[2] http://creativecommons.org/licenses/by-sa/2.0/
(CC BY-ND 2.0)[3] http://creativecommons.org/licenses/by-nd/2.0/

Printed and bound in the UK by Charlesworth Press.

CONTENTS

INTRODUCING N5 ACCOUNTING

Accounting is often defined as 'the language of business'. Accountants aim to collect, classify, organise, analyse, present and communicate financial information to the owners of business organisations and other interested stakeholders. Accounting is one of the oldest and most respected professions in the world, and accountants can be found in every industry from entertainment to medicine.

This National 5 Study Guide will help you to understand and interpret both financial and management accounting information and will equip you with the necessary skills to prepare a range of accounting statements. It will also help you to develop and apply skills for learning, skills for work and skills for life.

N5 COURSE CONTENT

The National 5 course contains three main units of study:

Preparing Financial Information (National 5)

This unit will focus on the role of financial accounting. You will gain an understanding of the purpose of a range of business documents and how these provide information which can be used to prepare double-entry ledger accounts. You will also develop an understanding and acquire the skills necessary to prepare the final accounting statements of a sole trader (trading and profit and loss account and balance sheet) in accordance with financial accounting concepts. Finally, this unit will help develop an understanding of year-end adjustments for accruals and prepayments as well as the accounting procedures for recording the depreciation of fixed assets.

Preparing Management Information (National 5)

This unit will focus on the role of management accounting. You will develop the knowledge and understanding of internal accounting information and the ability to prepare such information, using a range of basic accounting techniques. The information produced will be used by management in making decisions about the future planning and control of the business.

There will be a focus on the main elements of cost – materials (stock control), labour remuneration, overhead analysis and the preparation of job costing statements. In addition, this unit will develop the knowledge and skills necessary for effective budgetary control and break-even analysis.

Analysing Accounting Information (National 5)

In this unit, you will develop the skills, knowledge and understanding relating to the interpretation and analysis of accounting information. The information will be used to assess the organisation's current financial position and performance and assist with decision-making and future planning. This unit will focus particularly on ratio analysis and profit maximisation under conditions of a limiting factor.

COURSE ASSESSMENT: INTERNAL ASSESSMENT

Each of the three course units above will have a formal unit assessment. Unit assessments will require you to prepare accounting statements as well as be able to apply knowledge and understanding of key accounting concepts. All internal assessments will be undertaken in accordance with SQA assessment specifications. All unit assessments will be marked as a pass or a fail.

COURSE ASSESSMENT: EXTERNAL ASSESSMENT

Question Paper

The question paper will have **100 marks** and 10% of these will be allocated to theoretical questions. You will be expected to attempt **all** questions. This will be an end-of-course examination paper set by the SQA. The examination paper has two sections:
- **Section one** will have **60 marks** and will contain computational and theoretical questions
- **Section two** will have **40 marks** and will contain computational and theoretical questions.

The question paper will be a closed-book assessment and you will not know in advance what areas of the course content will be assessed.

contd

Assignment

The assignment will have **50 marks**. It will require you to work through a series of tasks to prepare accounting information and financial statements using a spreadsheet. You may be required to use this information to aid decision-making, analyse the organisation's financial position or to make recommendations for the future.

The assignment will make appropriate use of spreadsheets. You will be required to enter data with accuracy, and select and use appropriate formulae, formatting and printing functions to present information and accurately complete all accounting work.

HOW THIS BOOK CAN HELP YOU

This Study Guide (supported by the Digital Zone) explains clearly and precisely all the financial and management accounting concepts you need to know and understand to pass the internal and external elements of the National 5 Accounting course. It also has a wide range of challenging tasks and activities which provide you with the opportunity to develop your accounting skills.

The Study Guide will also ensure that the following generic skills for learning, life and work are fully developed:

- Numeracy
- ICT
- Decision-making
- Presentation
- Analysing
- Evaluating
- Thinking
- Employability
- Enterprise
- Analytical

While you complete all coursework tasks and activities manually on paper, you will make use of spreadsheet software as well. Tasks and activities can be completed following the templates shown throughout this Study Guide and the Digital Zone.

The new Scottish Curriculum for Excellence advocates providing you with the opportunity to work independently to develop a deeper understanding of areas of learning that interest you. Some extension material has been included to challenge you and further develop your interest in the subject. Extension material will not be examined by SQA at National 5 level. However, it will be useful if you plan to go on to study Accounting at Higher level.

INTERNATIONAL ACCOUNTING STANDARDS (IAS)

Adoption of International Accounting Standards (IAS) requires a change in the terminology used in the preparation of the final accounts of business organisations. Whilst there are no compulsory requirements for the presentation of the accounts of **sole traders** to use IAS, it is recommended that you become familiar with preparing all accounting statements in the IAS format. This will ensure you are well prepared if you are progressing to study Accounting at SQA Higher level or at college or university.

Throughout this Study Guide key terminology used in the preparation of accounting statements are presented using IAS terminology. The most frequently used IAS terminology used at National 5 is listed below.

International Accounting Terminology	
Non-current assets	Carrying amount
Inventory	Non-current liabilities
Trade receivables	Income statement
Other receivables	Statement of financial position
Trade payables	Cost of sales
Sales	Property
Allowance for doubtful debts	Profit for the year

PREPARING FINANCIAL ACCOUNTING INFORMATION

SOLE TRADERS

A sole trader is the name given to a business owned by one person. Examples of sole traders could include businesses like newsagents, hairdressers, grocer shops, taxi drivers or cafes and restaurants.

ADVANTAGES OF BEING A SOLE TRADER

- The owner gets to keep all the profits – so there is the opportunity to earn a lot of money.
- The owner gets to make all the decisions on how to run the business – they are their own boss.

DISADVANTAGES OF BEING A OF SOLE TRADER

- It involves a lot of hard work and the owner may find it difficult to get time off or have a holiday.
- Sometimes the owner has to do all the work on his/her own – there is no one there to help or offer advice or expertise.
- The owner will be responsible if the business does not do well and incurs losses. The owner could actually lose his/her personal belongings, for example their house or car, to pay off the business's debts.
- As a sole trader is a smaller firm, they have fewer assets to secure a loan on.

RAISING FINANCE

A sole trader will probably need some money of his/her own to start up the business. However, they may also need to raise money in the form of a loan from a bank or building society.

When a sole trader borrows money from a bank or building society, they have to be sure that they can make regular monthly payments to pay the money back and of course they are likely to be charged interest.

SOURCES OF FINANCE

Sources of finance include:

- Loans from family and friends
- Loans from banks or building societies
- Government grants
- Enterprise grants, for example, from the Prince's Trust.

The table on page 7 shows some advantages and disadvantages of these sources of finance.

contd

Source of finance	Advantages	Disadvantages
Grant	This is money given to a business by central or local government, the EU or from the Prince's Trust for things such as the purchase of new machinery or training of staff. It is often used to persuade businesses to locate in areas of high unemployment. It doesn't have to be paid back.	Grants can be complicated to apply for and the business often needs to meet many conditions before they are awarded the grant. Grants are usually one-off payments.
Retained profits	An established business will usually 'hold' or retain profit from previous years in the business. Retained profits can be used to buy more stock or to take advantage of bulk buying, which should increase future profits.	When a business has to continually use retained profits to solve short-term cash flow problems, it is often unable to grow and expand.
Bank loan	A bank loan is usually granted for a fixed amount, and has to be paid back in fixed monthly instalments over a fixed period of time – for example, five years. The business can budget for the monthly repayments and is able to purchase essential machinery or equipment straightaway.	Interest has to be paid in addition to the loan itself. New and relatively small businesses might find it difficult to convince lenders to give them a loan.
Trade credit	Trade credit allows a business to buy goods and pay for them at a later date. This gives the business time to sell stock at a higher price and earn a profit before the bill from the supplier has to be paid.	Cash discount for prompt payment to suppliers is likely to be lost. If payment is not made within the agreed credit period, suppliers will be reluctant to offer credit to the business in the future.
Hire purchase	Hire purchase allows a business to buy an asset, such as a delivery van, and pay it back over a fixed period of time – for example, 36 months. An initial deposit is required, followed by monthly payments. This allows a business to purchase expensive equipment with only an initial deposit.	The business does not legally own the asset until the last hire purchase payment has been made. If interest rates are high, then this can be an expensive form of borrowing.
Owner's personal finance	This includes using personal savings or borrowing money from family and friends who are willing to support the business. The main advantage is that borrowing is reduced and the owner(s) maintain control of the business.	All of these savings and this money could be invested in a business that does not succeed. It's a risk for those involved. Owners could lose all their capital.
Mortgage	A common method of financing the purchase of (property) land and premises is to take a mortgage from a bank, where a long-term loan is secured against the title deeds for the land or buildings of a property. The bank or other mortgage provider retains ownership of the land or premises until the entire mortgage has been repaid. The business is generally given a long period of time (20–25 years) to repay the mortgage.	If the borrower doesn't meet the monthly mortgage repayments, the lender can claim ownership of the property and sell it to retrieve the money they lent the business. Interest is charged for the duration of the mortgage in addition to the actual mortgage repayments. This can be very expensive.
Loan from family and friends	Families are more likely to offer lower rates of interest and perhaps offer longer repayment terms.	The sole trader may not be able to repay family and friends if the business does not succeed and this could cause problems with personal relationships.

ONLINE

Head to www.brightredbooks.net/N5Accounting to find out more about various Prince's Trust loans.

THINGS TO DO AND THINK ABOUT

Consider the advantages and disadvantages of the sources of finance listed above. If you were to start out as a sole trader, which source(s) would you opt for and why?

STATEMENTS OF FINANCIAL POSITION

THE STATEMENT OF FINANCIAL POSITION – THEORY

All businesses usually prepare a statement of financial position at least once per year. A statement of financial position is a STATEMENT which shows the value of the assets, liabilities and equity of a business.

Non-current Assets

These are large items owned by the business and which are likely to be in the business for many years. They are likely to be items of high value. Examples of non-current assets include: property, machinery, motor vehicles, fixtures and fittings and office equipment, and they should be entered into the statement of financial position in descending order of value, that is: property, machinery, fixtures and fittings, office equipment and motor vehicles.

Without non-current assets the business would probably not be able to operate.

Current Assets

These are smaller items of value owned by a business which will be kept for less than one full year. Their value changes from day to day. For example, if you sell inventory to customers for cash, the value of inventory will reduce and the amount of cash will increase.

Examples of current assets include: inventory, trade receivables, cash and cash equivalents.

Current Liabilities

These are items owed by the business and they will normally have to be repaid in the short-term, that is within one year. Examples of current liabilities include: bills payable, bank overdrafts and trade payables.

Long-term Liabilities

These are long-term debts of the business and will usually take many years to repay. Examples of long-term liabilities include: large loans (£100 000) from banks to purchase property or expensive machinery and mortgages. The business will have repay a certain amount each year over a 10–20 year period.

Equity

This is the money (or other assets) provided by the owner in order to start the business. This is sometimes referred to as NET WORTH – how much the business is worth when all liabilities have been paid.

TRADE RECEIVABLES AND TRADE PAYABLES

What is a Trade Receivable?	What is a Trade Payable?
A trade receivable is another business or person who owes the business money.	A trade payable is another business or person who the business owes money to.
Trade receivables are current assets because they will be expected to pay their debt within one year, that is the current financial year.	Trade payables are current liabilities as the business will be expected to make payment within one year, that is within the current financial year.

DON'T FORGET

Remember the importance of good presentation when creating a statement of financial position – use a ruler. You should also double check all your calculations using a calculator.

DON'T FORGET

Both sections of the statement of financial position must agree! Non-current assets, when added to net current assets, should agree with capital invested and long-term liabilities.

ONLINE TEST

How well have you learned this topic? Head to www.brightredbooks.net/N5Accounting and take the test.

10 STEPS FOR PREPARING A STATEMENT OF FINANCIAL POSITION

All statements of financial position should be displayed as shown below. They should be presented neatly and all calculations should be accurate.

Step 1	Write the name of the business and the title "Statement of Financial Position as at (appropriate date)".
Step 2	List all of the non-current assets – start with the most expensive non-current asset. Once you have them all listed, total them.
Step 3	List all of the current assets – they should be listed in order of liquidity, for example, inventory, trade payables, cash and cash equivalents. Once you have them all listed, total them.
Step 4	List all of the current liabilities. Total the current liabilities and transfer the total to the column containing the current assets.
Step 5	Subtract current liabilities from your current assets and transfer the answer to the non-current asset column. This figure should then be labelled net current assets/working capital.
Step 6	Add net current assets/working capital to the total non-current assets. You have now completed the first half of the statement of financial position.
Step 7	Enter the heading "Financed by".
Step 8	Under this heading place your capital figure.
Step 9	Enter the heading "Long-term liabilities". List your long-term liabilities below your capital figure.
Step 10	Add capital and long-term liabilities together.

EXAMPLE: (IAS) Traditional Terminology

John Bannerman
Statement of Financial Position as at 31 December 20.

Non-current Assets	£	£	£
Property			100 000
Machinery			90 000
Equipment			40 000
Motor Vehicles			20 000
			250 000
CURRENT ASSETS			
Inventory		25 000	
Debtors		15 000	
Cash and Cash Equivalents		15 000	
		55 000	
CURRENT LIABILITIES			
Trade Payables	5 000		
Bills Payable	3 000		
Overdraft	2 000	10 000	
Net Current Assets/Working Capital			45 000
			295 000
FINANCED BY			
Capital			200 000
LONG-TERM LIABILITIES			
Loan			95 000
			295 000

THINGS TO DO AND THINK ABOUT

Answer the following questions in sentences on A4 lined paper.

		Marks
1	Outline the purpose of preparing a statement of financial position.	1
2	Explain what is meant by non-current assets.	2
3	List 4 examples of non-current assets.	4
4	Explain what is meant by a current asset.	2
5	List 4 examples of current assets.	4
6	Explain what is meant by a trade receivable.	1
7	Explain what is meant by current liabilities.	2
8	Explain what is meant by a trade payable.	1
9	What is a bank overdraft?	1
10	Explain what is meant by the term net current assets.	2
11	Explain, using an example, what is meant by long-term liabilities.	2

PREPARING A STATEMENT OF FINANCIAL POSITION

PREPARING STATEMENTS OF FINANCIAL POSITION USING A SPREADSHEET

EXAMPLE:

	A	B	C	D	E	F
1	L Dawson					
2	Statement of Financial Position as at 31 May 20..					
3				£	£	£
4	NON-CURRENT ASSETS					
5	Property					10 000
6	Fixtures					5 000
7	Vehicles					4 000
8						=sum(F5:F7)
9						
10	CURRENT ASSETS					
11	Inventory				2 000	
12	Trade Receivables				1 500	
13	Cash and Cash Equivalents				500	
14					=sum(E11:E13)	
15						
16	CURRENT LIABILITIES					
17	Trade Payables			2 000		
18	Bills Payable			100	=sum(D17:D18)	
19	NET CURRENT ASSETS					=E14-E18
20						=F8+F19
21						
22	FINANCED BY					
23	Equity					20 900
24						
25						
26						

- To total a range of numbers we use the formula =sum(F5:F7)
- To add two numbers we use the simple formula =F8+F19
- To subtract two numbers we use the formula =E14-E18

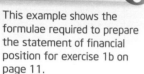

DON'T FORGET

This example shows the formulae required to prepare the statement of financial position for exercise 1b on page 11.

DON'T FORGET

Non-current assets should be shown in order of value, that is the highest valued non-current asset should be shown first and then the next highest in value should be shown second and so on.

DON'T FORGET

Current assets should be listed in order of liquidity – inventory, trade receivables, cash and cash equivalents.

EXERCISES ON STATEMENTS OF FINANCIAL POSITION

EXERCISE 1

(a) Copy the table below into your worksheet then prepare the statement of financial position of L Dawson as at 31 May 20.. from the following information:

(Identify the section of the statement of financial position where each item will be included by placing a tick in the appropriate column).

Item	Non-current Asset	Current Asset	Current Liability	Financed By
Equity £9 900				
Property £5 000				
Motor Vehicles £4 000				
Trade Receivables £1 000				
Inventory £1 500				
Cash and Cash Equivalents £500				
Loan £100				
Trade Payables £2 000				

(b) Open the spreadsheet template BSSS.

Enter the details from Exercise 1 under the appropriate heading.

Insert appropriate formulae to undertake all calculations.

Insert your name, exercise 1b and today's date in the footer.

Save the document as Ex1bss and print one copy.

EXERCISE 2

(a) Copy the table below into your worksheet then prepare the statement of financial position of J McDonald as at 30 November 20.. from the following information:

(Identify the section of the statement of financial position where each item will be included by placing a tick in the appropriate column).

Item	Non-current Asset	Current Asset	Current Liability	Financed By
Equity £20 000				
Loan £1 000				
Property £10 000				
Fittings £4 000				
Inventory £3000				
Trade Receivables £2 000				
Cash and Cash Equivalents £2 000				

(b) Open the spreadsheet template BSSS.

Enter the details from Exercise 2 under the appropriate heading.

Insert appropriate formulae to undertake all calculations.

Insert your name, exercise 2b and today's date in the footer.

Save the document as Ex2bss and print one copy.

THINGS TO DO AND THINK ABOUT

All organisations will have some non-current assets. Think about:

1. Schools
2. Hospitals
3. Supermarkets
4. Local corner shops
5. Libraries
6. Health Clubs

Provide two examples of non-current assets that would appear on the statements of financial position of the organisations shown above.

You yourself are likely to have some personal non-current assets. Write down three examples of non-current assets that you possess.

Finally, remember that practice makes perfect – the more you practice preparing statements of financial position, the more likely you are to succeed in your National 5 Accounting course.

ONLINE TEST

Test your knowledge of preparing statements of financial position at www.brightredbooks.net/N5Accounting

ONLINE

For more practice activities on preparing statements of financial position, head to www.brightredbooks.net/N5Accounting

CALCULATING NET WORTH

At any point in time we can calculate the net worth or equity invested in a business by subtracting all the business's liabilities from the total of all their business's assets.

HOW TO CALCULATE NET WORTH

⚙ EXERCISE 1

Copy and complete the table below completing the missing figures:

Assets	Liabilities	Net Worth
20 000	?	5 000
?	10 000	20 000
45 000	15 000	?
80 000	?	60 000

⚙ EXERCISE 2

(a) Using the information given below write up the statement of financial position of Sandra Smith as at 15 June 20..

Calculate the missing equity figure.

	£
Equipment	5 000
Property	35 000
Fixtures and Fittings	4 600
Motor Vehicles	16 000
Trade Receivables	10 000
Trade Payables	900
Cash and Cash Equivalents	12 300
Machinery	2 000
Inventory	3 500
Equity	?

DON'T FORGET ✚

Assets – Liabilities = Net Worth or Capital

(b) Open the spreadsheet template BSSS.

Enter the details from Exercise 2 under the appropriate heading.

Insert appropriate formulae to undertake all calculations.

Insert your name, exercise 2b and today's date in the footer.

Save the document as Ex2bss and print one copy.

⚙ EXERCISE 3

	£
Inventory	760
Trade Receivables	700
Property	45 000
Machinery	6 500
Fixtures and Fittings	12 300
Trade Payables	2 100
Cash and Cash Equivalents	880
Bank Overdraft	150
Motor Vehicles	6 340
Loan	100
Equity	?

(a) Using the information below write up the statement of financial position of B Thomson as at 18 June 20..

Calculate the figure for capital.

(b) Open the spreadsheet template BSSS.

Enter the details from Exercise 3 under the appropriate heading.

Insert appropriate formulae to undertake all calculations.

Insert your name, exercise 3b and today's date in the footer.

Save the document as Ex3bss and print one copy.

contd

EXERCISE 4

(a) Using the information given below write up the statement of financial position of L Marshall as at 12 December 20..

Calculate the missing figure for equity.

	£
Property	25 000
Equipment	5 000
Cash Register	350
Fixtures and Fittings	2 500
Cash and Cash Equivalents	4 000
Inventory	3 250
Trade Payables	1 800
Bank Overdraft	460
Motor Vehicles	3 200
Machinery	2 000
Loan	245
Equity	?

(b) Open the spreadsheet template BSSS. Enter the details from Exercise 4 under the appropriate heading.

Insert appropriate formulae to undertake all calculations.

Insert your name, exercise 4b and today's date in the footer.

Save the document as Ex4bss and print one copy.

 ONLINE

Learn more about statements of financial position by following the link at www.brightredbooks.net/N5Accounting

SUMMARY

A statement of financial position is simply a list of a business's ASSETS and LIABILITIES at a particular point in time.
We know that:
ASSETS – LIABILITIES = NET WORTH
In other words, if you simply add up all the assets of a business and take away all the liabilities, you will know the net value of the business, or how much the business is worth.

 ## THINGS TO DO AND THINK ABOUT

Businesses are involved in financial transactions all the time, for example, purchasing inventory from suppliers, selling inventory to customers, buying new assets such as motor vehicles, and using cash to pay bills such as electricity and telephone.

It would take too much time to produce a new statement of financial position after every transaction – businesses would be producing many statements of financial position every day!

 ONLINE TEST

Test your knowledge of preparing statements of financial position at www.brightredbooks.net/N5Accounting

DOUBLE-ENTRY BOOKKEEPING 1

DOUBLE-ENTRY BOOKKEEPING: AN OVERVIEW

Double-entry bookkeeping is an art which developed hundreds of years ago. Merchants and traders (shop keepers) kept a large book where the details of the amounts owed or owing, and the value of non-current and current assets were kept.

This book was called a ledger. Each page in the ledger was called an account because it told the story or 'gave an account' of when new assets were purchased and for

how much; and why certain amounts of money were owed and to whom they were owed. Today most double-entry bookkeeping is undertaken using modern technology, for example spreadsheet software.

So instead of producing a statement of financial position after every transaction, businesses use ledger accounts to keep a record of all transactions.

DON'T FORGET

The simple rule of double-entry bookkeeping is:
Each **DEBIT** entry must have a corresponding **CREDIT** entry.

EXAMPLE:

If a business bought a car using money in the bank, the ledger accounts would look like this:

Car A/c

Date	Details	Dr	Cr	Balance
3 Oct 20..	Bank	3000		3000 (Dr)

Bank A/c

Date	Details	Dr	Cr	Balance
1 Oct 20..	Balance			5000 (Dr)
3 Oct 20..	Motor Vehicle		3000	2000 (Dr)

The above transaction shows that £3000 has been taken out of the bank (the bank balance has been reduced from £5000 to £2000) and used to buy a motor vehicle. The current asset bank has been reduced and we now have a fixed asset of motor vehicle worth £3000.

THE CAPITAL ACCOUNT

One of the first ledger accounts that you will usually be required to open is for equity. Equity is the money used to start a business. It is usually deposited into the businesses bank account in order to allow the business to start buying assets and paying for expenses.

EXAMPLE:

If Jake Milne started up in business on 1 September 20.. as a sole trader by depositing his equity of £20000 into a bank account, the ledger accounts would be as follows:

Equity A/c

Date	Details	Dr	Cr	Balance
1 Sep 20..	Bank		£20000	£20000

Bank A/c

Date	Details	Dr	Cr	Balance
1 Sep 20..	Equity	£20000		£20000

As you can see, the bank a/c has been debited with £20000 and there is a corresponding credit in the equity for £20000.

KEY LEARNING POINT

Remember these rules for posting to ledger accounts:

Debit	The accountant should always debit:					
Assets	Increases in assets	Money coming into cash or bank	Purchases of inventory	Sales returns	Expenses	Drawings
Credit	The accountant should always credit:					
Liabilities	Increases in liabilities	Money going out of bank or cash	Equity	Sales	Purchases returns	

contd

It is now time for you to develop your skills in double-entry bookkeeping.

EXAMPLE:

The table below has three columns. The first column shows a number of financial transactions. The next two columns show which accounts would be debited and credited to record each of these transactions.

Transaction	Debit	Credit
Started business with £10 000 in a bank account.	Bank £10 000	Equity £10 000
Bought motor vehicle £2000 paying by cheque.	Motor Vehicle £2000	Bank £2000
Bought machinery £3000 paying by cheque.	Machinery £3000	Bank £3000
Withdrew £600 in cash from the bank.	Cash £600	Bank £600
Introduced further capital of £2000 into the bank.	Bank £2000	Equity £2000
Transferred £200 worth of cash into the bank.	Bank £200	Cash £200
Received a loan of £4000 that was paid into the bank account.	Bank £4000	Loan £4000
Bought a computer £1200 paying by cheque.	Computer £1200	Bank £1200

THE TRIAL BALANCE

At regular intervals (at least once a year) it is necessary to check the accuracy of your LEDGER ACCOUNTS to ensure that every DEBIT has a corresponding CREDIT as well as checking that your arithmetic is correct.

A trial balance is simply a list of all the DEBIT account balances in one column and all the CREDIT account balances in another column. If our ledger accounts have been posted correctly (with no arithmetical errors), then the total of the two columns should agree – or BALANCE. Look at the example shown below:

EXAMPLE: J Bannerman

Trial Balance as at 31 December 20 ..	£ Dr	£ Cr
Sales Revenue		2 500
Purchases	1 200	
Equity		10 000
Motor Vehicle	5 300	
Machinery	6 000	
	12 500	12 500

A trial balance could be prepared on a spreadsheet as shown below:

	A	B	C	D	E	F
1	J Bannerman					
2	Trial Balance as at 31 December 20..					
3					£	£
4	Sales Revenue					2 500
5	Purchases				1 200	
6	Equity					10 000
7	Motor Vehicle				5 300	
8	Machinery				6 000	
9					=sum(E4:E8)	=sum(F4:F8)
10						

DON'T FORGET

If both sides of the trial balance fail to agree then there are likely to be errors in one or more ledger accounts.

ONLINE

Learn more about ledgers by following the link at www.brightredbooks.net/N5Accounting

ONLINE TEST

Test your knowledge of ledgers at www.brightredbooks.net/N5Accounting

VIDEO

Learn more about double-entry bookkeeping by watching the video at www.brightredbooks.net/N5Accounting

THINGS TO DO AND THINK ABOUT

You should consider the advantages of using a spreadsheet to record your ledger accounts. Load a blank spreadsheet file on your computer and design a template using appropriate formulae which will automatically calculate the balance on each ledger account as each account is debited or credited.

Now you can complete the activities on the next two pages manually on paper or electronically on the spreadsheet file you have created.

ONLINE

For more great activities on double-entry bookkeeping, head to www.brightredbooks.net/N5Accounting

DOUBLE-ENTRY BOOKKEEPING 2

PURCHASES

When a business buys inventory from a supplier (e.g. a cash and carry) that will be resold to customers this is known as **PURCHASES**. A purchases account is opened and an entry is made to record each time a purchase of inventory takes place. Purchases may be paid for in cash or by credit. Purchases are nearly always bought on credit and so the business will now have a **TRADE PAYABLE**.

EXAMPLE:

A sole trader purchased inventory (£5000) 0n 2 April 20.. from Bulk Buy Cash and Carry. The double-entry would be recorded as follows:

Purchases A/c

Date	Details	Dr	Cr	Balance
2 Apr 20..	Bulk Buy Cash and Carry	£5000		£5000 (Dr)

Bulk Buy Cash and Carry (Trade Payable) A/c

Date	Details	Dr	Cr	Balance
2 Apr 20..	Purchases		£5000	£5000 (Cr)

PURCHASES RETURNS

Sometimes inventory purchased will have to be returned to the supplier. This could be for a number of reasons, for example: faulty, damaged, wrong colour or the wrong amount of inventory was ordered or delivered.

When inventory is returned to the supplier this is known as **PURCHASES RETURNS** and these are recorded in a separate purchases returns account.

EXAMPLE:

On 5 April 20.. the sole trader above returned £1000 of the goods purchased on 2 April 20.. to Bulk Buy Cash and Carry as they were damaged. The double-entry would be recorded as follows:

Purchases Returns A/c

Date	Details	Dr	Cr	Balance
5 Apr 20..	Bulk Buy Cash and Carry		£1000	£1000 (Cr)

Bulk Buy Cash and Carry (Trade Payable) A/c

Date	Details	Dr	Cr	Balance
2 Apr 20..	Purchases		£5000	£5000 (Cr)
5 Apr 20..	Purchases Returns	£1000		£4000 (Cr)

DOUBLE-ENTRY FOR SALES AND SALES RETURNS

When the business sells its inventory this is known as (SALES REVENUE) **SALES** or **TURNOVER**. Each time a sale is made this is recorded in a sales account. The business may sell the goods and ask for cash payment or they may be prepared to sell the goods on credit and accept payment later. When the business sells on credit they will now have a **TRADE RECEIVABLE**.

contd

EXAMPLE:

J Bannerman is a sole trader and on 6 April 20.. sells goods worth £2100 on credit to S Craig. The double-entry would be recorded as follows:

Sales A/c

Date	Details	Dr	Cr	Balance
6 Apr 20..	S Craig		£2100	£2100 (Cr)

S Craig (Trade Receivable) A/c

Date	Details	Dr	Cr	Balance
6 Apr 20..	Sales	£2100		£2100 (Dr)

SALES RETURNS ACCOUNT

Sometimes inventory sold will be returned by the customer. This could be for a number of reasons, for example:

Wrong colour, damaged, faulty or the wrong amount was ordered or delivered.

When customers return goods to the business this is known as **SALES RETURNS** and these are recorded in a separate sales returns account.

EXAMPLE:

On 8 April 20.. S Craig returned £200 of the goods that J Bannerman sold to her on 6 April 20.. The double-entry would be recorded in the ledger of J Bannerman as follows:

Sales Returns A/c

Date	Details	Dr	Cr	Balance
8 Apr 20..	S Craig	£200		£200 (Dr)

S Craig (Trade Receivable) A/c

Date	Details	Dr	Cr	Balance
6 Apr 20..	Sales	£2100		£2100 (Dr)
8 Apr 20..	Sales Returns		£200	£1900

ONLINE

For more practice activities on debits and credits, head to www.brightredbooks.net/N5Accounting

ONLINE TEST

Test your knowledge of debits and credits at www.brightredbooks.net/N5Accounting

DON'T FORGET

Every debit must have a corresponding credit.

THINGS TO DO AND THINK ABOUT

Joseph Sedgewood started business on 1 September 20.. with equity made up of £3000 in the bank and equipment worth £300. Copy the table below and indicate which account should be credited and which account should be debited.

Date	Details of Transaction	Account to be Debited	Account to be Credited
2 September	He obtained a loan of £500 from J Morton and put this into his bank account.		
3 September	Purchased more equipment by cheque £600.		
4 September	Inventory for resale was purchased by cheque £220.		
4 September	Took £240 from the bank for cash use.		
5 September	Sold goods for £60 cash.		
10 September	Some purchases of 4 September were returned to suppliers and a cheque for £75 was received.		
12 September	More goods were sold for cash £40.		
14 September	Customers returned faulty goods sold on 5 September and were paid out £18 cash.		

Record all of the above transactions into the appropriate ledger accounts in the ledger of Joseph Sedgewood and prepare a trial balance at 14 September.

FURTHER EXERCISES ON DOUBLE-ENTRY BOOKKEEPING

EXERCISE 1

Horace Jonson started business on 1 March 20.. with equity of £4000 in a bank account. This should be shown in his ledger accounts at that date. Several transactions then took place. Copy the table below and indicate which account should be credited and which account should be debited.

Date	Details of Transaction	Account to be Debited	Account to be Credited
2 March	He purchased shop fittings by cheque £480.		
3 March	He took £1000 from the bank for business use.		
5 March	Inventory was purchased for cash £250.		
5 March	Cash sales £85.		
7 March	Further inventory was purchased by cheque £560.		
8 March	Some of the goods bought on 5 March were unsuitable and returned. A cheque for £40 was received.		
10 March	Cash sales £100.		

Record all of the above transactions into the appropriate ledger accounts in the ledger of Horace Jonson and prepare a trial balance.

EXERCISE 2

Freda Lawrence decided to start a business buying and selling craft items in the local market. Copy the table below and indicate which account should be credited and which account should be debited.

Date	Details of Transaction	Account to be Debited	Account to be Credited
1 June	Started business with equity of £200 cash.		
2 June	Purchased inventory for £70.		
3 June	Opened bank account by putting £80 cash into bank.		
3 June	Sold goods for £90 cash.		
5 June	Obtained loan from her bank, £300, which was put into her bank account.		
6 June	Purchased more goods by cheque £140.		
7 June	Some goods sold on 3 June worth £10 were of poor quality and returned.		
10 June	She paid part of the loan by cheque £100.		

Record all of the above transactions into the appropriate ledger accounts in the ledger of Freda Lawrence and prepare a trial balance.

EXERCISE 3

Isaac Brown started business in January 20.. and asks you to show how his accounts would appear in the ledger. Copy the table below and indicate which account should be credited and which account should be debited.

Date	Details of Transaction	Account to be Debited	Account to be Credited
1 January	Put £2000 in a bank account as equity.		
3 January	Purchased goods for resale £520 by cheque.		
4 January	Took £100 out of bank for cash use.		
8 January	Sold goods for £230 and received cash.		
11 January	Brown returned some previously purchased goods and received a cheque for £40.		
13 January	Sold goods for £210.		
14 January	Some of the goods sold on 8 January were returned as unsuitable and £360 cash was paid out.		

Record all of the above transactions into the appropriate ledger accounts in the ledger of Isaac Brown and prepare a trial balance.

EXERCISE 4

Herbert Floss opened a record shop in the town centre. Copy the table below and indicate which account should be credited and which account should be debited. Open up ledger accounts to show the following transactions.

Date	Details of Transaction	Account to be Debited	Account to be Credited
1 April	Started business with equity made up of £200 in cash and £6000 in a bank account.		
2 April	Purchased goods for resale by cheque £800.		
3 April	Cash sales £400.		
4 April	Goods sold, cheque received £80.		
5 April	Shop fittings purchased by cash £200.		
6 April	Goods purchased by cash £350.		
9 April	Floss paid out a cheque for £95 when some of the inventory sold on 3 April was returned by customers.		
12 April	£100 was transferred from bank to cash.		

Record all of the above transactions into the appropriate ledger accounts in the ledger of Herbert Floss and prepare a trial balance on the last date.

 contd

EXERCISE 5

Susan Glover started business on 1 October 20.. with the aim of buying and selling t-shirts. Copy the table below and indicate which account should be credited and which account should be debited. Show her ledger accounts.

Date	Details of Transaction	Account to be Debited	Account to be Credited
1 October	Opened business with premises worth £7000 and money in the bank £2000.		
2 October	Transferred £300 from the bank to cash.		
4 October	Purchased inventory from Auto Agents PLC £1200 and paid by cheque.		
5 October	Obtained a loan from A Watson by cheque £600.		
6 October	Sold some inventory for cash £92.		
7 October	Sold goods £126. Cheque received.		
13 October	Some of the goods purchased on 4 October were returned as unsuitable. A cheque for £186 was received.		
14 October	Purchased further inventory from Auto Agents PLC by cheque £736.		
16 October	Customer M Graham returned some faulty goods and was given £30 cash. .		

Record all of the above transactions into the appropriate ledger accounts in the ledger of Susan Glover and prepare a trial balance on the last date.

 THINGS TO DO AND THINK ABOUT

Now that you are familiar with the principles of double-entry bookkeeping, try this assessment task.

ASSESSMENT TASK

W Sethi opened a car accessories business on 1 March with £2500 in the bank and £500 cash. Copy the table below and indicate which account should be credited and which account should be debited.

Date	Details of Transaction	Account to be Debited	Account to be Credited
1 March	Bought shop fittings £340 by cheque.		
1 March	Purchased goods for resale £800 by cheque.		
4 March	Cash sales £200.		
8 March	Paid wages in cash £120.		
8 March	Customer returned car vacuum (electrical fault) and £46 cash was issued.		
11 March	Withdrew £150 from bank for own use.		
14 March	Bought inventory for cash £200.		
15 March	Paid wages in cash £120.		
18 March	Cash sales £380.		
20 March	Bought filing cabinet and accessories £250 and paid by cheque.		
28 March	Withdrew £50 cash for own use.		

Record all of the above transactions into the appropriate ledger accounts for W Sethi and draw up a trial balance at the end of March.

 DON'T FORGET

Every debit must have a corresponding credit.

ONLINE

For more practice activities on double-entry bookkeeping, head to www.brightredbooks.net/N5Accounting

 ONLINE TEST

Test your knowledge of double-entry bookkeeping at www.brightredbooks.net/N5Accounting

THE TRIAL BALANCE

REVISION

The purpose of a trial balance is to check the accuracy of your double-entry bookkeeping. Every debit entry should have a corresponding credit entry and therefore if both sides of a simple trial balance agree, it can be assumed that the trial balance is arithmetically correct.

When preparing a trial balance remember the following principles:

Debit Side (Dr)	Credit Side (Cr)
Assets	Equity
Expenses	Liabilities
Purchases	Sales
Sales returns	Purchases returns
Drawings	Monies received
Discount allowed	Discount received

 **EXERCISE 1**

(a) Prepare the trial balance of P Newman as at 31 December 20.. and insert the missing equity figure.

	£
Sales Revenue	12 200
Purchases	11 850
Wages	1 756
General Expenses	2 280
Sales Returns	125
Equipment	6 780
Premises	28 750
Trade Payables	677
Trade Receivables	28
Cash and Cash Equivalents	908
Opening Inventory	400
Equity	?

(b) Open the spreadsheet template TBSS.
Enter details from Exercise 1 under the appropriate heading.
Use auto sum (Σ) to total both sides of the trial balance.
Insert your name, exercise 1b and today's date in the footer.
Print one copy of your spreadsheet showing formulae.
Save the document as Ex1bTB and print one copy.

EXERCISE 2

(a) Prepare the trial balance of Janet Anderson as at 31 December 20.. and insert the missing equity figure.

	£
Sales Revenue	45 000
Trade Receivables	7 250
Insurance	965
Purchases	27 890
Trade Payables	8 900
Premises	50 000
Rent Received	250
Inventory at 1 January	8 343
Wages	10 000
Drawings	4 450
Equity	?

(b) Open the spreadsheet template TBSS.
Enter details from Exercise 2 under the appropriate heading.
Use auto sum (Σ) to total both sides of the trial balance.
Insert your name, exercise 2b and today's date in the footer.
Print one copy of your spreadsheet showing formulae.
Save the document as Ex2bTB and print one copy.

EXERCISE 3

(a) Prepare the trial balance of John Lock as at 31 December 20.. and insert the missing equity figure.

	£
Premises	90 000
Drawings	2 300
Rent	125
Opening Inventory	1 000
Cash and Cash Equivalents	350
Purchases	12 000
Trade Payables	2 500
Purchases Returns	300
Sales Revenue	58 000
Trade Receivables	4 000
Telephone	125
Discount Received	100
Equity	?

(b) Open the spreadsheet template TBSS.
Enter details from Exercise 3 under the appropriate heading.
Use auto sum (Σ) to total both sides of the trial balance.
Insert your name, exercise 3b and today's date in the footer.
Print one copy of your spreadsheet showing formulae.
Save the document as Ex3bTB and print one copy.

contd

 **EXERCISE 4**

(a) Prepare the trial balance of Alastair Murray as at 30 September 20.. and insert the missing equity figure.

	£
Purchases	3500
Carriage In	250
Bank Overdraft	1700
Inventory	610
Carriage Out	180
Sales Revenue	6400
Sales Returns	130
Trade Receivables	290
Wages	950
Discount Received	110
Trade Payables	220
Drawings	1800
Equipment	4000
Equity	?

(b) Open the spreadsheet template TBSS. Enter details from Exercise 4 under the appropriate heading.
Use auto sum (Σ) to total both sides of the trial balance.
Insert your name, exercise 4b and today's date in the footer.
Print one copy of your spreadsheet showing formulae.
Save the document as Ex4bTB and print one copy.

EXERCISE 5

(a) Prepare the trial balance of Cameron McTaggart as at 31 December 20.. and insert the missing equity.

	£
Purchases	4100
Carriage In	300
Sales Returns	290
Purchases Returns	400
Carriage Out	190
Bank Overdraft	1200
Discount Allowed	1060
Trade Receivables	5900
Sales Revenue	6200
Trade Payables	2100
Bank Charges	320
Rent Received	250
Equity	?

(b) Open the spreadsheet template TBSS. Enter details from Exercise 5 under the appropriate heading.
Use auto sum (Σ) to total both sides of the trial balance.
Insert your name, exercise 5b and today's date in the footer.
Print one copy of your spreadsheet showing formulae.
Save the document as Ex5bTB and print one copy.

 THINGS TO DO AND THINK ABOUT

Answer TRUE or FALSE to each of the following questions:

1. Non-current assets always appear on the debit side of a trial balance.
2. Current assets always appear on the credit side of a trial balance.
3. Purchases always appear on the credit side of a trial balance.
4. Sales revenue always appears on the debit side of a trial balance.
5. Liabilities like loans always appear on the credit side of a trial balance.
6. Drawings always appear on the credit side of a trial balance.
7. Equity always appears on the credit side of a trial balance.
8. Sales revenue always appears on the debit side of a trial balance.
9. Purchases always appear on the debit side of a trial balance.
10. When a trial balance fails to agree, this indicates that there is likely to be one or more errors in the ledger accounts.

 DON'T FORGET

The debit column and the credit column of the trial balance should agree!

 DON'T FORGET

Add up the debit column, then add up the credit column – capital is the difference between the two columns and should appear on the credit side of the trial balance.

 ONLINE

For more practice activities on the trial balance, head to www.brightredbooks.net/N5Accounting

 ONLINE TEST

Test your knowledge of the trial balance at www.brightredbooks.net/N5Accounting

 DON'T FORGET

Using a spreadsheet with appropriate formulae is more efficient than using a calculator to total long columns of numbers!

BUSINESS DOCUMENTS: INVOICES

Purchaser

Supplier

| Letter of enquiry sent by the purchaser to potential supplier |
| Order sent by the purchaser |
| Cheque sent by the purchaser |

| Quotation or price list sent by the supplier |
| Invoice sent by the supplier |
| Credit note sent by the supplier if goods were returned |
| Statement sent by the supplier each month to summarise each months transactions |

THE DOCUMENT TRAIL

The diagram below shows the documents which are commonly used when one business buys goods from another business.

All business documents are used as records but only the following documents are used by the Accounts Department for double-entry accounting purposes:

- Invoices
- Credit notes
- Cheques
- Statements.

INVOICE

This is another name for a 'bill'. An invoice is a detailed list of the goods purchased and is sent by the seller to the buyer when the goods are sent out. A **copy** of the invoice will be prepared at the same time. The copy invoice will be used by the seller to make the necessary entries into their own sales revenue and trade receivables account.

An invoice provides us with information to write up our ledger accounts. Look at the invoice below:

ONLINE

Head to www.brightredbooks.net and check out the 'Business Documents' presentation.

INVOICE

Mr A Andrews
East Nile Street
Dundee
DD7 9PS

To: **Bannerman Trading**
High Street
Hightown
HT4 8ST

Tel No: 011 67345

Invoice No 1

VAT No: 231 8763 24

Date 20 August 20..

QUANTITY	DESCRIPTION	UNIT PRICE	COST
		£	£
2	Boxes of batteries	15·00	30·00
5	Rolls of film	4·00	20·00
			50·00
		LESS Trade Discount (10%)	5·00
		Net Goods Value	45·00
		ADD **VAT** (20%)	9·00
			54·00

Trade Discount

This is a **reduction in the catalogue price** offered to encourage customers to buy from this supplier rather than another supplier. Trade discount is given to customers who frequently buy from the same supplier or who buy in bulk.

VAT

VAT stands for Value Added Tax. This is a government tax on goods – paid by the purchaser of the goods. The current rate is 20%. The seller simply collects the VAT from the purchaser and passes it on to the government. The firm collecting the VAT does not keep it!

RULES FOR RECORDING INVOICES IN THE LEDGER

Debit purchases with the net goods value

Debit VAT with the amount of VAT charged

Credit the trade payable account with the total invoice value

| EXAMPLE: | Ledger of Bannerman Trading Company |

Purchases A/c

Date	Details	Dr	Cr	Balance
20 Aug 20..	A Andrews	£45		£45 (Dr)

Vat A/c

Date	Details	Dr	Cr	Balance
20 Aug 20..	A Andrews	£9		£9 (Dr)

A Andrews A/c

Date	Details	Dr	Cr	Balance
20 Aug 20..	(Purchases and VAT)		£54	£54

THINGS TO DO AND THINK ABOUT

Try the following task on completing an invoice.

(a) Bannerman Trading received the following invoice from Jim Morrice. Looking at the invoice you will see that Bannerman Trading received a Trade discount of 10% as they are a loyal and valued customer.

On A4 paper or in your workbook, you should open the appropriate ledger accounts in the ledger of Bannerman Trading and show how this invoice would be recorded in these ledger accounts.

INVOICE	To: **Bannerman Trading**
Jim Morrice	**High Street**
South Street	**Hightown**
Aberdeen	**HT4 8ST**
AB7 9PS	

Tel No: 011 67345   Invoice No: 1

VAT No: 231 8763 24   Date 8 January..

QUANTITY	DESCRIPTION	UNIT PRICE	COST
		£	£
4	Large Frames	6·00	24·00
4	Medium Frames	4·50	18·00
4	Small Frames	3·25	13·00
			55·00
	LESS **Trade Discount** (10%)		5·50
	Net Goods Value		49·50
	ADD **VAT** (20%)		9·90
			59·40

BUSINESS DOCUMENTS: COPY INVOICES

WHAT IS A COPY INVOICE?

When an invoice is sent to a customer, this is to 'bill' them for purchases made. Before the invoice is sent to the customer, the seller will keep a copy of it (copy invoice) as this will provide a **record of his/her sales**. Look at the copy invoice shown below:

EXAMPLE:

COPY INVOICE

Bannerman Trading
High Street
Hightown
HT4 8ST

Tel No: 011 67345   Copy Invoice No 1

VAT No: 231 8763 24   Date: 25 August 20..

To: Easyprint Plc.
    Lochend Road
    Chateaulait
    CH4 1AT

QUANTITY	DESCRIPTION	UNIT PRICE	COST
		£	£
50	Memory Cards	2·00	100·00
5	Boxes of Batteries	10·00	50·00
			150·00
	LESS Trade Discount (20%)		30·00
	Net Goods Value		120·00
	ADD VAT (20%)		24·00
			144·00

In most cases, duplicate documents/paper are used with the invoice being on the top and the copy invoice behind. The top copy (invoice) can be sent to the buyer and the bottom copy (copy invoice) retained by the seller as a record of their sales.

In addition, the invoice and the copy invoice will probably be in different colours.

Recording a Copy Invoice in the Ledger

The rule for recording copy invoices (sales) in the ledger of a sole trader is:

Credit sales with the net goods value

Credit VAT with the amount of VAT charged

Debit the trade receivable account with the total invoice value

contd

EXAMPLE: Ledger of Bannerman Trading

Sales Revenue A/c

Date	Details	Dr	Cr	Balance
25 Aug 20..	Easyprint Plc.		£120	£120 (Cr)

Vat A/c

Date	Details	Dr	Cr	Balance
25 Aug 20..	Easyprint Plc.		£24	£24 (Cr)

Easyprint Plc. A/c

Date	Details	Dr	Cr	Balance
25 Aug 20..	(Sales and VAT)	£144		£144 (Dr)

THINGS TO DO AND THINK ABOUT

Study the copy invoice shown below. Bannerman Trading sent the original invoice to Foto Express and kept a copy invoice to allow them to record the information in their own ledger accounts.

On A4 paper or in your workbook, you should open the appropriate ledger accounts in the ledger of Bannerman Trading and show how this copy invoice would be recorded in these ledger accounts.

COPY INVOICE

Bannerman Trading
High Street
Hightown
HT4 8ST

Tel No: 011 67345   **Copy Invoice No 2**

VAT No: 231 8763 24   Date: 4 May 20..

To: Foto Express
25 Argyle Street
Motherwell
ML1 6QT

QUANTITY	DESCRIPTION	UNIT PRICE	COST
		£	£
20 Bottles	Developing Fluid	2·50	50·00
5 Boxes	Printing Paper	5·00	25·00
			75·00
	LESS Trade Discount (20%)		15·00
	Net Goods Value		60·00
	ADD VAT (20%)		12·00
			48·00

DON'T FORGET

When posting to the ledger, **sales revenue** is always placed on the **credit** side of the **sales revenue** account.

DON'T FORGET

VAT on all sales revenue is also placed on the **credit** side of the **VAT** account.

ONLINE

For another practice activity on completing a copy invoice, head to www.brightredbooks.net/N5Accounting

ONLINE TEST

Test your knowledge of copy invoices at www.brightredbooks.net/N5Accounting

BUSINESS DOCUMENTS: CREDIT NOTES

WHAT IS A CREDIT NOTE?

Once an invoice has been sent it **cannot** be changed. If an error is discovered the supplier will send the buyer a **credit note**. A credit note will be issued if:
- the supplier has made a mistake and charged too much;
- the goods were damaged on delivery;
- the wrong or unsuitable goods have been supplied.

A credit note is also used as evidence that goods have been returned and is an acknowledgement that the returned goods have been received. Credit notes **reduce the amount** due by the supplier.

EXAMPLE:

CREDIT NOTE

**Easyprint plc
Lochend Road
Chateaulait
CH4 1AT**

Tel No: 011 67345

VAT No: 231 8763 24

Credit Note No 1

Date 10 May 20..

**To: Bannerman Trading
    High Street
    Hightown
    HT4 8ST**

QUANTITY	DESCRIPTION	UNIT PRICE	COST
		£	£
1	Boxes of batteries (**wrong size**)	15·00	15·00
2	Memory cards (**damaged**)	4·00	8·00
			23·00
	LESS Trade Discount (10%)		2·30
	Net Goods Value		20·70
	ADD VAT (20%)		4·14
			28·84

RECORDING A CREDIT NOTE IN THE LEDGER

The rule for recording credit notes (purchases returns) in the ledger of a sole trader:

Credit purchases returns with the net goods value

Credit VAT with the amount of VAT charged

Debit the supplier account with the total credit note value

contd

EXAMPLE:

The credit note on page 26, sent by A Andrews to Bannerman Trading would be posted in the ledger of Bannerman Trading as follows:

Ledger of Bannerman Trading

Purchases Returns A/c

Date	Details	Dr	Cr	Balance
10 May	A Andrews		£20.70	£20.70 (Cr)

Vat A/c

Date	Details	Dr	Cr	Balance
10 May	A Andrews		£4.14	£4.14 (Cr)

A Andrews A/c

Date	Details	Dr	Cr	Balance
10 May	Purchases Returns and VAT	£24.84		£24.84

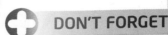

DON'T FORGET

When posting to the ledger, **purchases returns** are always placed on the **credit** side of the **purchases returns account**.

DON'T FORGET

VAT on all **purchases returns** is also placed on the **credit** side of the **VAT** Account

THINGS TO DO AND THINK ABOUT

Study the credit note shown below. Bannerman Trading returned goods to Pamela Steel Ltd. They had been sent the wrong goods. They received this credit note from Pamela Steel Ltd.

On A4 paper or in your workbook, you should open the appropriate ledger accounts in the ledger of Bannerman Trading and show how this credit note would be recorded in these ledger accounts

CREDIT NOTE

**Pamela Steel Ltd
Wynd Avenue
Manchester
MM9 3IL**

Tel No: 011 67345   **Credit Note No 2**

VAT No: 231 8763 24   Date 19 September 20..

**To: Bannerman Trading
  High Street
  Hightown
  HT4 8ST**

QUANTITY	DESCRIPTION	UNIT PRICE	COST	
		£		£
1 ream	Copy Paper	4·00		4·00
				4·00
	LESS Trade Discount (10%)			0·40
	Net Goods Value			3·60
	ADD VAT (20%)			0·72
				4·32

ONLINE

For another practice activity on completing a credit note, head to www.brightredbooks.net/N5Accounting

ONLINE TEST

Test your knowledge of credit notes at www.brightredbooks.net/N5Accounting

BUSINESS DOCUMENTS: COPY CREDIT NOTES

WHAT IS A COPY CREDIT NOTE?

Before a credit note is sent out a copy is taken. This is then called a copy credit note and is used by the business to record all sales returns. Look at the example shown below:

EXAMPLE:

COPY CREDIT NOTE

**Bannerman Trading
High Street
Hightown
HT4 8ST**

Tel No: 011 67345

Copy Credit Note No 1

VAT No: 231 8763 24

Date: 10 October 20..

To: Easyprint Plc.
Lochend Road
Chateaulait
CH4 1AT

QUANTITY	DESCRIPTION	UNIT PRICE	COST
		£	£
2	Memory Cards (damaged)	2·00	4·00
			4·00
	LESS Trade Discount (20%)		0·80
	Net Goods Value		3·20
	ADD **VAT** (20%)		0·64
			3·84

In most cases duplicate documents/paper are used with the credit note being on the top and the copy credit note behind. The top copy (credit note) can be sent to the buyer who has returned the goods and the bottom copy (copy credit note) retained by the seller as a record of their sales returns.

In addition, the credit note and the copy credit note will probably be in different colours.

RECORDING COPY CREDIT NOTES IN THE LEDGER

The rule for recording copy credit notes (sales returns) in the ledger of a sole trader:

Debit sales returns with the net goods value

Debit VAT with the amount of VAT charged

Credit the trade receivable account with the total copy credit note value

contd

EXAMPLE: Ledger of Bannerman Trading

Sales Returns A/c

Date	Details	Dr	Cr	Balance
10 Oct 20..	Easyprint Plc.	£3.20		£3.20 (Dr)

Vat A/c

Date	Details	Dr	Cr	Balance
10 Oct 20..	Easyprint Plc.	£0.64		£0.64 (Dr)

Easyprint Plc. A/c

Date	Details	Dr	Cr	Balance
10 Oct 20..	Sales Returns and VAT		£3.84	£3.84 (Cr)

THINGS TO DO AND THINK ABOUT

Study the Copy Credit Note shown below. Foto Express returned goods to Bannerman Trading. Bannerman Trading sent a Credit Note to Foto Express and kept this copy to allow them to record the appropriate information in their own ledger accounts

On A4 paper or in your workbook, you should open the appropriate ledger accounts in the Ledger of Bannerman Trading and show how this Credit Note would be recorded in these ledger accounts.

```
COPY CREDIT NOTE

                        Bannerman Trading
                           High Street
                           Hightown
                            HT4 8ST

Tel No: 011 67345            Copy Credit Note No 2

VAT No: 231 8763 24           Date 3 June 20..

To: Foto Express
    Argyle Street
    Motherwell
    ML1 6QZ
```

QUANTITY	DESCRIPTION	UNIT PRICE	COST
		£	£
1 ream	Copy Paper	2·50	2·50
			2·50
	LESS Trade Discount (20%)		0·50
	Net Goods Value		2·00
	ADD VAT (20%)		0·40
			2·40

ONLINE

For another practice activity on completing a copy credit note, head to www.brightredbooks.net/N5Accounting

ONLINE TEST

Test your knowledge of copy credit notes at www.brightredbooks.net/N5Accounting

DON'T FORGET

A copy credit note is used to record sales returns – the sales returns account is debited, VAT is debited and the personal account of the trade receivable is credited.

BUSINESS DOCUMENTS: CHEQUES AND CHEQUE COUNTERFOILS

WHAT ARE CHEQUES AND CHEQUE COUNTERFOILS?

When goods are bought and sold on credit, payment is often made by **cheque**. A cheque is a document that orders the payment of money from a bank account – usually a current account. The **purchaser** (in response to invoices received) will write a cheque (stating the amount in money and words, date of payment and the name of the payee) for the amount he owes the seller. He will sign the cheque and forward it as a means of making payment. This is really an order to his bank to pay the person/business named on the cheque.

Upon receiving the cheque, the **seller** will update their records by **debiting** the bank account with the amount shown on the cheque. They will also **credit** the trade receivable account (with the amount shown on the cheque) as they have now made a payment.

The **purchaser** will also complete a cheque counterfoil at the same time as the cheque is prepared. Cheque counterfoils provide a record of all payments made from a bank account. When the purchaser sends a cheque to pay the seller, he will use the cheque counterfoil to complete his own double-entry, that is:

1. Credit bank account
2. Debit the supplier account.

ONLINE

For practice activities on preparing business documents, head to www.brightredbooks.net/N5Accounting

ONLINE TEST

Test your knowledge of cheques and cheque counterfoils at www.brightredbooks.net/N5Accounting

EXAMPLE:

Examples of a cheque and cheque counterfoil are shown below.

Date __09 June 2015__
To __Office Demisters__
For __1 Air Conditioner__
Balance bt _____
Deposit _____
Balance _____
This cheque __£570.00__
Balance ct _____
0000105

ABC Bank *Business Account*
ABC Bank, 100 High St, Main Road, London, UK, SW10 2NO   Date __09 June 2015__
Not transferable
Pay __Office Demisters__
__Five Hundred and Seventy Pounds only__   £ __570.00__
Handyman Hardware Store

Cheque number	Sort code	Account number
0000105	01-02-03	123456789

COUNTERFOIL   CHEQUE

DON'T FORGET

The key business documents used for recording double-entry financial transactions in the ledger are:
- Invoices
- Copy invoices
- Credit notes
- Copy credit notes
- Cheques
- Cheque counterfoils

SUMMARY

INVOICE	COPY INVOICE
Dr Purchases Account	Cr Sales Revenue Account
Dr VAT Account	Cr VAT Account
Cr Trade Payable Account	Dr Trade Receivable Account

CREDIT NOTE	COPY CREDIT NOTE
Cr Purchases Returns Account	Dr Sales Returns Account
Cr VAT Account	Dr VAT Account
Dr Trade Payable Account	Cr Trade Receivable Account

THINGS TO DO AND THINK ABOUT

Study the credit note shown below. This credit note was sent to Corbit Cars on 5 July 20.. from a business called Motopartz.

Motopartz would **keep a copy of the credit note** to record the transaction in their own ledger accounts.

On a sheet of A4 paper or in your workbook, you should open the appropriate ledger accounts in the ledger of Motopartz and show how the information in the (copy) credit note would appear in the ledger of Motopartz.

DON'T FORGET

You would take a copy of the credit note prior to sending it to Corbit Cars.

Credit Note

Motopartz
2 Kilmaurs Road
Inverness
IV16 5DA

Telephone: 01382 825812   Credit Note Number: 155

VAT Number: 625 2193 55

Date: 5 July 20..

To: Corbit Cars
    57 Swanston Avenue
    Inverness
    IV10 7BZ

QUANTITY	DESCRIPTION	GOODS (PER UNIT)	VAT (20%)	TOTAL
		£	£	£
2	Brake Pipes	35·00	7·00	84·00
4	Oil Filters	6·00	1·20	28·80
		£94·00	£18·80	£112·80

Answer the following questions on A4 paper or in your workbook.

1. Suggest two reasons why Corbit Cars might have returned these items to Motopartz.

2. Suggest two reasons why Motopartz might allow its customers a trade discount.

CALCULATING TRADE DISCOUNT, CASH DISCOUNT AND VALUE ADDED TAX

WHAT IS A DISCOUNT?

A discount is a reduction in the price of goods. Two types of discount offered are:

Trade Discount

A trade discount is a **reduction** on the catalogue price of goods being sold and is offered by a seller to a buyer because they are a good customer, because they buy in bulk or because the seller wants them to come back and buy more.

Cash Discount

A cash discount is an additional discount on how much has to be paid – it is offered by the seller to encourage their customers to **pay promptly** – usually within one month.

DON'T FORGET

VAT rates can change.

VALUE ADDED TAX (VAT)

Value added tax is a tax used by the government and is added to the value of most goods and services provided by suppliers. **VAT is calculated on the lowest possible price to be paid for the goods**.

VAT is currently charged at the rate of 20% and is added by the supplier to the net goods value to calculate the invoice price of the goods being sold. The supplier acts as a **COLLECTOR** on behalf of the government. At regular intervals, the supplier will offset the VAT collected against the VAT paid and either send or receive a cheque to/from the government for the net amount.

EXAMPLE: 1

Cost price of goods	£1000
Add VAT at 20%	£200
Total amount due	£1200

⚙ VAT EXERCISE 1

Copy and complete the following table into your workbook and show the VAT calculation and invoice price payable for the following goods. The first one has been completed for you.

Cost Price	Vat (20%)	Invoice Price
£800	£160	£960
£2400		
£3800		
£4260		
£5320		
£6500		

When **trade discount** is offered, VAT is calculated on the goods price less the trade discount.

EXAMPLE: 2

Calculate the discount to find the net goods value (NGV), then calculate the VAT charged on the NGV and add the VAT to the NGV to find the invoice price.

Cost of goods	£1000
Less 20%	
Trade discount	£200
Vat (20%)	£160
Invoice price	£960

⚙ VAT EXERCISE 2

Copy and complete the following table into your workbook and show the VAT calculation and invoice price payable for the following goods. The first one has been completed for you.

Cost Price	Trade Discount %	Trade Discount Amount	Net Goods Value	Vat 20%	Invoice Price
£600	20%	£120	£480	£96	£576
£1500	15%				
£3200	10%				
£5480	20%				
£8264	25%				
£10000	20%				
£12500	10%				
£26200	5%				
£900	10%				

CALCULATING VAT WITH CASH DISCOUNT

When cash discount is offered, VAT is calculated on the goods price less the cash discount. Remember VAT is always calculated on the **lowest possible** price.

However, the cash discount will only be given if the invoice is paid within the time stated – usually one month. The seller will not know if the invoice will be paid within one month at the point when it is being prepared to be sent to the buyer. However, when calculating VAT we assume that they will pay within one month so VAT would be calculated as follows:

EXAMPLE: 3

```
INVOICE
                        Jim Morrice
                        South Street
                        Aberdeen
                        AB7 9PS

Tel No: 011 67345              Invoice No: 1

VAT No: 231 8763 24            Date 8 January ..

To: Bannerman Trading
    High Street
    Hightown
    HT4 8ST
```

QUANTITY	DESCRIPTION	UNIT PRICE	COST
		£	£
1	Cost price of goods	1000·00	1000·00
	Less 10% cash discount		100·00
	Net Goods Value		900·00
	ADD VAT (£900 x 20%) *		180·00
	Invoice Price (£1000 + £180)		1 180·00

*If the buyer pays within one month they will receive a £100 cash discount for prompt payment and so will only pay £900. So VAT of 20% would be calculated on £900 and not £1000.

EXAMPLE: 4

Cost of goods	£1 000
Less 10% trade discount	£100
Net goods value	£900
Less 10% **cash discount**	£90
Add VAT	
(£900–£90 = £810 x 20%)	£162
Invoice price	£1 062

 DON'T FORGET

VAT is always calculated on the **lowest possible** price.

ONLINE

For other practice activities on calculating trade discount, cash discount and value added tax, head to www.brightredbooks.net/N5Accounting

ONLINE TEST

Test your knowledge of calculating trade discount, cash discount and value added tax at www.brightredbooks.net/N5Accounting

 ## THINGS TO DO AND THINK ABOUT

Complete the following table to show the final invoice price after cash discount and VAT have been taken into account. The first one has been started for you.

Cost price	Cash discount %	Cash discount amount	Discounted price (cost – cash discount)	VAT on discounted price 20%	Invoice price (cost price + VAT)	Amount to be paid if paid within discount terms	Amount to be paid if not paid within discount terms
£6000	20%	£1200	£4800	£960	£6960	£6960	£7200
£750	25%						
£4000	40%						
£8500	20%						
£6200	30%						

When trade and cash discount are allowed VAT, is calculated on the lowest price the customer could pay. Calculate the discounts first and then calculate VAT on the lowest possible price.

ASSESSMENT TASKS

TRANSACTIONS

Example	Document used to record transaction
Cash received from customers for goods sold	Cash register (till) receipt
Paid rent by cash	Cash receipt would be issued by the landlord
Trade receivable paid amount owing	Cheque
Paid amount owing to trade payable	Cheque counterfoil
Purchased goods from supplier	Invoice
Sold goods to customer	Copy invoice
Returned goods to supplier	Credit note
Customer returned goods as damaged	Copy credit note

 EXERCISE 1

Part A

Sam's Sports Shop returned one Victor driver and three Deluxe Flight golf bags to Golfers' Haven because they were damaged in transit.

Using the information above and below, complete the credit note to be sent to Sam's Sports Shop on 21 April.

Golfers' Haven
Price List from March (excluding VAT)

Drivers

Mammoth	£275.00
Pro 1	£105.00
Victor	£170.00

Golf Bags

Deluxe Stand	£65.99
Deluxe Flight	£45.00
Tourer Flight	£29.99

Terms:
Trade discount 10%
Cash discount 5% one month
VAT at 20%
All prices include delivery

Credit Note

Golfers' Haven
123 Green Drive
EDINBURGH
EH3 7BB

Tel No: 0131-454634
Fax No: 0131-454671

No. 357/2

Date: 21 April 2015
Tax Point: 21:4:15
VAT No: 392 536 147

Sam's Sports Shop
23 Park Road
NAIRN
IV12 5TR

Quantity	Description	Unit Price (£)	Cost (£)

Total Value: £

contd

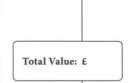

Part B

Golfers' Haven would keep a copy of the credit note to record the transaction in their ledger accounts. Show how the accounts would appear in the ledger of Golfers' Haven.

Ledger of Golfers' Haven

Sales Returns A/c

Date	Details	Dr	Cr	Balance

Vat A/c

Date	Details	Dr	Cr	Balance

Sam's Sports Shop A/c

Date	Details	Dr	Cr	Balance

DON'T FORGET

A trade discount is offered to regular customers or to customers who buy in bulk. A cash discount is offered to encourage prompt payment from debtors.

ONLINE TEST

Test your knowledge of recording business transactions at www.brightredbooks.net/N5Accounting

ASSESSMENT TASK 1

On 1 October 20.. J McDonald started business as a sole trader. Write up J McDonald's ledger in respect of the transactions shown below. VAT is charged at 20%.

October 1	J McDonald started in business with equity of £2000 in the bank and £500 in cash.
October 2	Purchased goods on credit from J Purdie £800.
October 2	Cash sales £200.
October 2	Paid £100 cash into bank.
October 3	Bought goods on credit from J Howitt £100.
October 5	Paid rent by cheque £60.
October 9	Cash sales £70.
October 14	Sent an invoice to T MacLean £330 less 2% trade discount (less 10% cash discount)
October 15	Sent back £15 worth of goods J Howitt.
October 17	Cash sales £30.
October 19	Paid £30 cash into bank.
October 22	Received a cheque from T MacLean for amount due less 10% cash discount.

Draw up J McDonald's trial balance at 31st December 20..

ASSESSMENT TASK 2

Show the ledger accounts of T Wallace at the end of December 20.. (VAT is charged at 20%)

December 1	Started business with equity of cash £270 bank £410.
December 1	Received an invoice from E Boyle £200 less 2% trade discount. (£15 cash discount)
December 2	Bought fixtures and fittings by cheque £135.
December 3	Cash sales £300.
December 4	Paid electricity by cheque £45.
December 5	Sent an invoice to Northern Supplies Ltd £400 less 3% trade discount.
December 6	Cash sales £145.
December 6	Paid £90 cash into bank.
December 7	Sold goods on credit to F Burns £500 less 3% trade discount.
December 8	Sent a credit note Northern Supplies £100.
December 10	Sold goods and received cheque £70.
December 11	Withdrew £50 cash for own use.
December 14	Bought goods on credit from R Smith £200 less 1% trade discount.
December 17	Sent a cheque to E Boyle to settle his account less £15 discount.
December 20	Received a credit note from R Smith £100.
December 20	Cashed a cheque for £20.

Draw up T Wallace's trial balance at 31 December 20...

THINGS TO DO AND THINK ABOUT

Working with a partner you should discuss the necessity for a business to operate a double-entry bookkeeping system for the recording of financial transactions. You should also outline the advantages of operating a double-entry system.

You may wish to present your findings in the form of a PowerPoint presentation.

STATEMENT OF ACCOUNT

WHAT IS A STATEMENT OF ACCOUNT?

At the end of each month, the seller of goods and services will send out a document called a statement of account to the buyer. A **statement of account** shows a summary of transactions that have taken place for a given period of time – usually one month. This allows the buyer to pay for his goods at the end of each month rather than write a cheque for each individual invoice received. It also shows a summary of all business transactions between the buyer and the seller.

The statement of account will show:

- any amount unpaid from the previous statement – the balance that the buyer still owes the seller from the previous month (or previous statement);
- all transactions that took place in a particular month, for example sales and sales returns;
- payments made;
- any discounts involved;
- balance outstanding at the end of the month.

GUIDELINES FOR PREPARING A STATEMENT OF ACCOUNT

Step 1	Statements are prepared by the seller and sent to the buyer – usually monthly.
Step 2	Record the opening balance in the statement – this is the amount the buyer owes to the seller from the previous month's business.
Step 3	Information is transferred from the debtors ledger account to the statement. For example, in the statement below, Alan Turing has sold goods to William Oswald. So William Oswald is Alan Turing's (trade receivable) debtor – hence the amount he owes for sales on April 5 is posted to the **debit side** of the statement that will be sent to William Oswald.
Step 4	When William Oswald makes a payment to Alan Turing or return goods to Alan Turing, this is recorded on the **credit side** of the statement. This shows that the amount William Oswald owes to Alan Turing has been reduced. For example, William Oswald pays Alan Turing on 15 April £345.45 by cheque and so this reduces the debit balance.
Step 5	At 15 April, William Oswald still has a debit balance of £140.58. This will appear as the opening balance in May's statement.

DON'T FORGET

Cash discount – A further reduction in the amount paid by the buyer of goods because he has paid his bill promptly.

ONLINE TEST

Test your knowledge of statements of accounts at www.brightredbooks.net/N5Accounting

STATEMENT OF ACCOUNT

Alan Turing
Riverside Drive
Dundee
DD1 4FT

To: William Oswald   VAT Reg No: 242 8567 52
   17 Stafford Street
   PAISLEY
   PA12 4TG   Date: 30 April

Date	Details	Debit	Credit	Balance
		£	£	£
April 1	Balance	351.45		351.45 (Dr)
April 5	Sales*	384.72		734.17 (Dr)
April 10	Sales returns		234.30	499.87 (Dr)
April 15	Bank		345.45	154.42 (Dr)
April 15	Discount allowed		6.40	140.02 (Dr)

*To calculate sales on April 5, when cash discount is allowed:
Sales £400 less trade discount (20%) £80 = net goods value £320
NGV £320 less cash discount (2%) £6.40 = £313.60
VAT = £313.60 x 20% = £62.72
SALES = £320 + £62.72 = £382.72

contd

EXERCISE 1

You are the Accounts Clerk for Catherine's Carpets and are responsible for sending out statements of account to customers each month.

(a) Complete the statement of account to be sent Holm Furnishers from the information below.

1 April: Holm Furnishers owed Catherine's Carpets £1 220.50.

2 April: Sold goods £780 (excluding VAT) to Holm Furnishers (25% trade discount is to be allowed and 10% cash discount is offered for payment within one month).

13 April: Received a cheque from Holm Furnishers for £1 160.25 in full settlement of amount outstanding on 1 April.

17 April: Holm Furnishers returned damaged goods previously purchased on 2 April – £154 (excluding VAT).

(b) Name the documents which would have been sent on 2 April and 17 April and state four pieces of information that would be included in each document.

(c) Explain the difference between cash and trade discount.

ONLINE

Head to the Digital Zone to download template statements of accounts for Exercises 1 and 2 and the Things to Do and Think About: www.brightredbooks. net/N5Accounting

EXERCISE 2

Complete the statement of account which Sandra Grant would send to Scotia Photography at the end of April from the information given below:

April 1: Sandra Grant was owed £699.75 by Scotia Photography.

April 5: Sold goods valued at £450 (excluding VAT) to Scotia Photography (20% trade discount was allowed and terms of payment were – cash discount 5%, 30 days).

April 14: A cheque was received from Scotia Photography for £669.75 in full settlement of the balance outstanding on 1 April.

April 19: Faulty goods valued at £87.46 (including VAT) were returned by Scotia Photography.

Name the document which would have been sent to Scotia Photography on 5 April 20..

Name the document which would have been sent to Scotia Photography on 19 April 20..

THINGS TO DO AND THINK ABOUT

Now that you have tried Exercises 1 and 2 above, have a go at the challenge below (remember that the template statement of accounts is on the Digital Zone at www.brightredbooks.net/N5Accounting):

R Young specialises in selling mathematical equipment.

Complete the statement of account sent to S Cahill on 30 April.

1 April: S Cahill owed R Young £360.

5 April: Sold goods on credit to S Cahill with a catalogue price of £600 (excluding VAT). Trade discount of 20% was allowed and a 2% cash discount for payment within one month.

10 April: Cahill returned damaged goods valued at £250 (including VAT).

15 April: A cheque was received from Cahill for £350 in full settlement of the balance outstanding on 1 April.

Name the documents that Young would send relating to the transactions on 5 April and 10 April.

FINAL ACCOUNTS 1

WHAT ARE FINAL ACCOUNTS?

The main reason why people set up in business as a sole trader is to make profits. However, if they are not successful they may well incur losses instead. The calculation of profit (or loss) is probably the most important objective of accounting. Usually once per year the sole trader will wish to prepare a set of final accounts. Final accounts consist of an:

● Income statement
● Statement of financial position

The figures used in the preparation of the income statement and statement of financial position are taken from the trial balance.

LAYOUT OF AN INCOME STATEMENT

The income statement shows the profit or loss made from purchasing goods at one price (the cost price) and selling them at a higher price (the selling price). The income statement is the first account prepared for a sole trading organisation. Look at the example of the first half of the income statement shown below.

EXAMPLE:

J Bannerman

Income statement for the year ended 31 December 20..			
	£	£	£
Sales Revenue			28 400.35
Less Sales Returns			349.50
Net Sales			28 050.85
Less Cost of Sales			
Opening Inventory		575.25	
Purchases	14 759.05		
Add Carriage In	316.90		
	15 075.95		
Less Purchases Returns	116.25	14 959.70	
		15 534.95	
Less Closing Inventory		2485.00	
			13 049.95
GROSS PROFIT			15 000.90

ONLINE

For more activities on final accounts, head to www.brightredbooks.net/N5Accounting

ONLINE TEST

Test your knowledge of final accounts at www.brightredbooks.net/N5Accounting

contd

⚙ EXERCISE 1

(a) From the following information prepare the income statement of J Wilson for the year ended 31 December 20..

(b) Open the spreadsheet template TASS.

Enter the details from Exercise 1 under the appropriate heading.

Insert appropriate formulae to undertake all calculations.

Insert your name, exercise 1b and today's date in the footer.

Save the document as Ex1bTA and print one copy.

	£
Sales Revenue	27 500
Purchases	15 350
Sales Returns	250
Purchases Returns	50
Inventory at 1 January 20..	1750
Inventory at 31 December 20..	1950
Carriage In	100

⚙ EXERCISE 2

(a) From the following information prepare the income statement of R Smith for the year ended 31 December 20..

(b) Open the spreadsheet template TASS.

Enter the details from Exercise 2 under the appropriate heading.

Insert appropriate formulae to undertake all calculations.

Insert your name, exercise 2b and today's date in the footer.

Save the document as Ex2bTA and print one copy.

	£
Inventory at 1 January 20..	1275
Inventory at 31 December 20..	3250
Sales Revenue	75 350
Purchases	46 400
Sales Returns	1260
Purchase Returns	1425
Carriage Inwards	200

⚙ EXERCISE 3

(a) From the following information prepare the income statement of L Donnelly for the year ended 31 December 20..

(b) Open the spreadsheet template TASS.

Enter the details from Exercise 3 under the appropriate heading.

Insert appropriate formulae to undertake all calculations.

Insert your name, exercise 3b and today's date in the footer.

Save the document as Ex3bTA and print one copy.

	£
Inventory at 1 January 20..	2400
Inventory at 31 December 20..	3250
Credit Sales	125 600
Cash Sales	35 200
Purchases	72 400
Sales Returns	2450
Purchase Returns	1475
Carriage inwards	50

THINGS TO DO AND THINK ABOUT

Once you have tried exercises 1–3 above, head to the Digital Zone and try out the further tasks.

FINAL ACCOUNTS 2

WHAT IS AN INCOME STATEMENT?

After the gross profit has been calculated in the first half of the income statement, the next step is to prepare the profit and loss section where any additional income will be added and all the current year's expenses deducted. The resulting figure is called the profit for the year.

Add Money Received

These are other items of income the business has received during the financial year from sources other than the buying and selling of goods. For example:

- rent received by the firm if they sub-let part of their premises to another business;
- discount received from suppliers for paying their accounts promptly;
- commission received by the firm for selling goods on behalf of another firm.

Business Expenses

The total expenses of running the business for the year will be listed, totalled and then deducted from the total net income. There are a large number of items which may appear in the **less expenses** section of the income statement including:

- rates
- insurance
- salaries
- electricity
- carriage outwards (delivery charges)
- salesmen's salaries and commission
- delivery van repairs
- interest on loans
- bank charges
- telephone costs
- discount allowed.

So the final trading and profit and loss account will look as follows.

LAYOUT OF AN INCOME STATEMENT

EXAMPLE:

J Bannerman

Income Statement for the year ended 31 December 20..			
	£	£	£
Sales Revenue			28 400.35
Less Sales Returns			349.50
Net Sales			28 050.85
Less Cost of Sales			
Opening Inventory		575.25	
Purchases	14 759.05		
Add Carriage In	316.90		
	15 075.95		

contd

Less Purchases Returns	116.25	14959.70	
		15534.95	
Less Closing Inventory		2485.00	
			13049.95
GROSS PROFIT			15000.90
Add Gains			
Discount Received			100.00
Rent Received			500.00
			15600.90
Less Expenses			
Electricity		400	
Advertising		300	
Carriage out		50	
Wages		2500	
Telephone		200	3450.00
PROFIT FOR THE YEAR			12150.90

DON'T FORGET

The trading section includes all items down to and including gross profit.

DON'T FORGET

The profit and loss section includes all items from gross profit down to profit for the year.

ONLINE TEST

Test your knowledge of income statements at www.brightredbooks.net/n5accounting

THINGS TO DO AND THINK ABOUT

Now try out the following exercises for yourself:

1. (a) From the information listed below, draw up the income statements of Tracey Turner for the year ended 31 December 20..

	£
Sales Revenue	1700
Sales Returns	95
Rent Received	450
Purchases	820
Purchases Returns	54
Opening Inventory	25
Closing Inventory	60
Insurance	25
Wages	32
Electricity	24

(b) Open the spreadsheet template TPLSS.

Enter the details from Exercise 1 under the appropriate heading.

Insert appropriate formulae to undertake all calculations.

Insert your name, exercise 1b and today's date in the footer.

Save the document as Ex1bTPL and print one copy.

2. (a) From the information listed below draw up the income statements of R Burton for the year ended 31 December 20..

	£
Sales Revenue	17033
Purchases	9101
Sales Returns	32
Purchases Returns	12
Opening Inventory	3521
Closing Inventory	3171
Insurance	130
Commission Received	1100
General Expenses	34
Telephone	146
Advertising	180

(b) Open the spreadsheet template TASS.

Enter the details from Exercise 2 under the appropriate heading.

Insert appropriate formulae to undertake all calculations.

Insert your name, exercise 2b and today's date in the footer.

Save the document as Ex2bTPL and print one copy.

PREPAYMENTS AND ACCRUALS

WHAT IS A PREPAYMENT?

This is where the business has **paid more** than it should have for the accounting period and so the amount actually paid has to be **reduced** in order to show what should have been paid. For example, if the business **paid £400** for telephone bills, but the actual telephone bill for the accounting year was £300, then the business has **prepaid by £100**.

The figure which would be charged to the income statement would be £300 (the actual cost of the telephone bill) and £100 would appear as a **prepaid expense** (other receivables) in the CURRENT ASSETS section of the business's statement of financial position.

ACCRUALS

This is where the business has **amounts owing** at the end of the accounting period and so the amount actually paid has to **be increased** in order to show what **should have been paid**. For example, if the business **paid £200** for cleaning expenses, but the actual cleaning expenses for the account year totalled **£400** then the business has **accrued expenses** (expenses owing) of **£200**.

The figure which would be charged to the income statement would be £400 (the actual cost of the cleaning expenses) and £200 would appear as an **accrued expense** (other payables) in the CURRENT LIABILITIES section of the statement of financial position.

DON'T FORGET +

A prepaid expense is a current asset; an accrued expense is a current liability!

 EXERCISE 1

(a) From the trial balance of J Alderton you are to prepare the income statement for the year ended 31 December 20..

	DR	CR
	£	£
Equity		151 410
Purchases	46 000	
Sales revenue		99 000
Purchase returns		300
Sales returns	700	
Discount allowed	800	
Discount received		600
Wages	20 600	
Salaries	10 100	
Rent	2 000	
Rates	1 800	
Carriage in	3 410	
Trade receivables	20 500	
Cash and cash equivalents	5 100	
Trade payables		35 100
Inventory	7 900	
Property	110 000	
Plant and machinery	54 000	
Motor vehicles	3 500	
	286 410	286 410

NOTES:

I.   Closing inventory was valued at £10 332
II. Wages were prepaid by £30
III. £18 salaries relates to next year
IV. Prepaid rent was £55
V.   £60 of rates were for next year

(b) Open the spreadsheet template TPLASS.

Enter the details from Exercise 1 under the appropriate heading.

Insert appropriate formulae to undertake all calculations.

Insert your name, exercise 1b and today's date in the footer.

Save the document as Ex1bTPLASS and print one copy.

contd

EXERCISE 2

From the following trial balance of A Knowles you are to prepare the income statement for the year ended 31 March 20..

	DR	CR
	£	£
Property	1 036 000	
Furniture and fittings	133 000	
Motor vehicles	335 000	
Equity		1 502 000
Trade receivables	163 000	
Trade payables		150 000
Cash ⎱ (Cash and cash	15 000	
Bank ⎰ equivalents)	31 000	
Wages and salaries	214 000	
Administrative expenses	24 000	
Vehicle expenses	17 000	
Building repairs	3 000	
Light and heat	21 000	
Sales revenue		836 000
Purchases	424 000	
Opening inventory	50 000	
Sales returns	4 000	
Purchase returns		3 000
Discount allowed	57 000	
Discount received		36 000
	2 527 000	2 527 000

NOTES:

I. The closing inventory was valued at £68 814.

II. Wages and salaries were prepaid by £110.

III. Administration expenses were prepaid by £96.

IV. £29 of lighting and heating refers to next year.

(b) Open the spreadsheet template TPLASS.

Enter the details from Exercise 2 under the appropriate heading.

Insert appropriate formulae to undertake all calculations.

Insert your name, exercise 2b and today's date in the footer.

Save the document as Ex2bTPLASS and print one copy.

ONLINE

Head online for more practice at preparing income statements at www.brightredbooks.net/N5Accounting

ONLINE TEST

Test your knowledge of prepayments and accruals at www.brightredbooks.net/N5Accounting

THINGS TO DO AND THINK ABOUT

Now that you've practiced preparing income statements in exercises 1 and 2, have a go at exercise 3!

3. (a) From the trial balance of W Washington and the notes which follow, you are asked to prepare the income statement for the year ended 30 September 20..

	DR	CR
	£	£
Equity		140 700
Commission received		500
Property	88 000	
Plant and machinery	23 000	
Fixtures and fittings	12 000	
Motor vehicles	8 000	
Purchases and sales revenue	75 000	156 000
Returns inwards and outwards	8 900	3 300
Carriage in	500	
Carriage out	800	
Administration expenses	32 000	
Trade receivables and trade payables	36 100	52 600
Inventory 1 October	25 000	
Discount received and allowed	10 000	5 700
Cash and cash equivalents	14 500	
Wages and salaries	25 000	
	358 800	358 800

NOTES:

I. Inventory on 30 September was valued at £10 000.

II. Wages and salaries were prepaid by £2000.

III. Administration expenses were prepaid by £4000.

(b) Open the spreadsheet template TPLASS.

Enter the details from Exercise 3 under the appropriate heading.

Insert appropriate formulae to undertake all calculations.

Insert your name, exercise 3b and today's date in the footer.

Save the document as Ex3bTPLASS and print one copy.

DEPRECIATION OF NON-CURRENT ASSETS

WHAT IS DEPRECIATION OF NON-CURRENT ASSETS?

Non-current assets have been defined as long-term assets, owned by the business for use in the business.

Most non-current assets have a limited life and fall in value over time. This fall in value of non-current assets is called depreciation. Depreciation of non-current assets occurs for a number of reasons. Non-current assets depreciate through:

- **Use** – as an asset is used, its value decreases.
- **Wear and tear** – use of machinery or vehicles or exposure to bad weather.
- **Time** – with the passage of time the asset decreases in value.
- **Obsolescence** – caused by advances in technology or changes in fashion, for example when new mobile phones come on to the market, older versions are usually replaced.

PROVISION FOR DEPRECIATION ACCOUNT

As the non-current asset loses value, its value must be decreased in the books of the business by writing off the reduction to a **provision for depreciation account**.

EXAMPLE:

C Chips decides to depreciate his motor vehicle by £2000 per year due to use. Here are the ledger accounts at the end of Year 1:

Motor Vehicle A/c

Date	Details	Dr	Cr	Balance
1 Jan 20..	Balance	10 000		10 000 (Dr)

Provision for Depreciation A/c

Date	Details	Dr	Cr	Balance
31 Dec 20..	Profit and Loss Account		2 000	2 000 (Cr)

At the end of the accounting year, the £2000 will then be **debited** (charged) to the income statement account as an expense.

STRAIGHT LINE METHOD

The straight line method of depreciation is where the same amount of depreciation is written off the asset each year. To calculate the depreciation to be charged annually, the accountant will deduct the scrap value of the asset from the cost of the asset, and divide the result by the estimated life of the asset.

Formula

$$\text{Annual depreciation} = \frac{\text{Cost of asset} - \text{Scrap value}}{\text{Estimated life of asset}}$$

 EXERCISE 1

From the following information, calculate the annual depreciation to be charged against the profits of L Yule for the following non-current assets purchased on 1 January Year 1. Yule uses the straight line method of depreciation.

	Asset	Cost (£)	Estimated Life	Residual/Scrap Value (£)
1	Machinery	200 000	5 years	20 000
2	Fixtures and Fittings	42 000	4 years	2 000
3	Office Equipment	20 000	3 years	2 000

Machinery depreciation = $\dfrac{£200\,000 - £20\,000}{5}$ = £36 000 per year

You should now calculate the depreciation for fixtures and fittings and office equipment in exactly the same way.

DEPRECIATION AND THE STATEMENT OF FINANCIAL POSITION

When we prepare the statement of financial position at the end of the financial year, all assets can now be shown at cost (how much the business paid for the assets when they were purchased new), the accumulated depreciation to date and the net book value of the asset at the statement of financial position date.

If you look at the example below, the statement of financial position clearly shows four non-current assets: property, machinery, equipment and motor vehicles.

The information in the statement of financial position will have been taken from the ledger accounts, similar to the ones you prepared in Exercise 1.

LAYOUT OF A STATEMENT OF FINANCIAL POSITION - REVISION

John Bannerman
Statement of Financial Position as at 31 December 20..

NON-CURRENT ASSETS	£	£	£
	Cost	Accumulated Depreciation	NBV
Property	120 000	20 000	100 000
Machinery	100 000	10 000	90 000
Equipment	45 000	5 000	40 000
Motor Vehicles	25 000	5 000	20 000
	290 000	40 000	250 000
CURRENT ASSETS			
Inventory		25 000	
Trade Receivables		15 000	
Bank } (Cash and Cash		10 000	
Cash } Equivalents)		5 000	
		55 000	
CURRENT LIABILITIES			
Trade Payables	5 000		
Bills owing	3 000		
Overdraft	2 000	10 000	
Net Current Assets/Working Capital			45 000
			295 000
FINANCED BY			
Equity			180 000
Add Profit for the year			20 000
			200 000
LONG-TERM LIABILITIES			
Loan			95 000
			295 000

ONLINE

Head online for more practice at preparing provision for depreciation accounts at www.brightredbooks.net/N5Accounting

ONLINE TEST

Test your knowledge of depreciation of non-current assets at www.brightredbooks.net/N5Accounting

DON'T FORGET

Depreciation is calculated annually and appears as an expense in the income statement. Accumulated depreciation (built up over several years) is shown in the statement of financial position.

THINGS TO DO AND THINK ABOUT

Anthony Delaporte is an artist specialising in portrait painting and picture framing.

From the following information, prepare his statement of financial position as at 31 March 20..

Your statement of financial position should balance at £50 700.

Equity	45 000
Premises	40 000
Equipment	7 350
Inventory	5 000
Trade Receivables	4 600
Bank Overdraft	1 200
Cash and Cash Equivalents	1 700
Trade Payables	6 400
Drawings	1 600
Profit for the year	7 300
Equipment Depreciation	350

FURTHER EXERCISES

EXERCISE 1

T Lundie extracted a trial balance on 31 march. From the information and notes that follow, prepare an income statement for year ended 31 March 20..

	DR £	CR £
Purchases and Sales Revenue	7620	13990
Inventory	1720	
Equity		6140
Bank overdraft		1450
Cash and Cash Equivalents	30	
Discount allowed and received	480	310
Returns in and Returns out	270	190
Carriage out	720	
Rent, rates and insurance	580	
Fixtures and fittings	500	
Delivery van	1000	
Provision for depreciation – fittings		300
Provision for depreciation – delivery van		300
Delivery van		100
Trade Receivables and Trade Payables	3970	2020
Wages and salaries	2980	
General office expenses	4930	
	24800	24800

NOTES:

1. Inventory at end was valued at £1430.
2. Wages and salaries accrued £70.
3. Rates prepaid £60.
4. A further 10% depreciation has to be written off the cost of fittings.
5. A further 5% depreciation has to be written off the cost of the delivery van.

EXERCISE 2

The following trial balance was extracted from the books of B Jones at the close of business on 28 February 20..

	DR £	CR £
Purchases and Sales Revenue	3760	6580
Bank Cash and Cash	380	
Cash Equivalents	70	
Equity		3300
Office furniture	600	
Provision for depreciation		
Office furniture		120
Rent and rates	860	
Discount allowed and received	230	120
Trade Receivables and Trade Payables	2590	920
Opening Inventory	990	
Delivery van	1340	
Provision for depreciation		
Delivery van		200
Van running costs	420	
	11240	11240

NOTES:

1. Closing inventory was valued at £1170.
2. Accrued van running costs amounted to £30.
3. Provision for depreciation on van and office furniture is to be 20% of cost.

From the information given above, prepare the income statement for the year ended 28 February.

EXERCISE 3

	DR £	CR £
Sales Revenue		100000
Inventory at Start	12000	
Purchases	70000	
Interest received		2000
Commission received		2000
Selling expenses	7000	
Office expenses	4000	
Rates	6000	
Sundry expenses	5000	
Property	95000	
Vehicles	30000	
Trade Receivables	12000	
Bank Cash and Cash	4000	
Cash Equivalents	1000	
Trade Payables		8000
Equity		142000
Drawings	8000	
	254000	254000

(a) From the following information, prepare the income statement of E Jones for year ended 31 March and a statement of financial position at that date.

NOTES:

1. The value of the closing inventory was £10000.
2. Selling expenses accrued amounted to £1500.
3. £500 of office expenses were still to be paid.
4. Depreciate vehicles by 10%.

(b) Open the spreadsheet template FASS.

Enter the details from Exercise 3 under the appropriate heading.

Insert appropriate formulae to undertake all calculations.

Insert your name, exercise 3b and today's date in the footer.

Save the document as Ex3bFASS and print one copy.

EXERCISE 4

(a) From the information below and the notes that follow, prepare the income statement of R Burniston for the year ended 31 December and a statement of financial position on that date.

	DR	CR
	£	£
Sales Revenue		150 000
Opening Inventory	25 000	
Purchases	100 000	
Carriage in	10 000	
Administration expenses	10 000	
Selling expenses	5 000	
Rates	3 000	
Financial expenses	2 000	
Premises at cost	50 000	
Motor vehicles at cost	10 000	
Provision for depreciation – Premises		5 000
Provision for depreciation – Motor vehicles		1 000
Trade Receivables	5 000	
Cash and Cash equivalents	3 000	
Trade Payables		4 000
Overdraft		2 000
Equity		66 000
Drawings	5 000	
	228 000	228 000

NOTES:

1. The value of closing inventory was £15 000.

2. Provide a further £5000 depreciation on premises.

3. Provide a further £4000 depreciation on motor vehicles.

(b) Open the spreadsheet template FASS.

Enter the details from Exercise 4 under the appropriate heading.

Insert appropriate formulae to undertake all calculations.

Insert your name, exercise 4b and today's date in the footer.

Save the document as Ex4FASS and print one copy.

 ONLINE

Head online for more practice at preparing income statements and statements of financial position at www.brightredbooks.net/N5Accounting

EXERCISE 5

(a) From the information shown below, prepare the income statement of Courtney-Thorne Smith for the year ended 31 August and a statement of financial position at that date.

TRIAL BALANCE OF COURTNEY-THORNE SMITH ON 31 AUGUST

	DR	CR
	£	£
Sales Revenue		80 000
Purchases	50 000	
Inventory at Start	8 000	
Rent and rates	2 000	
General expenses	15 000	
Selling expenses	3 000	
Premises	100 000	
Machinery	20 000	
Trade Receivables	20 000	
Cash and Cash Equivalents	10 000	
Trade Payables		7 000
Drawings	3 000	
Equity		144 000
	231 000	231 000

NOTES:

1. Closing inventory was valued at £5000.

(b) Open the spreadsheet template FASS.

Enter the details from Exercise 1 under the appropriate heading.

Insert appropriate formulae to undertake all calculations.

Insert your name, exercise 6b and today's date in the footer.

Save the document as Ex6bFASS and print one copy.

 ONLINE TEST

Test your knowledge of preparing income statements and statements of financial position at www.brightredbooks.net/N5Accounting

 DON'T FORGET

Profit for the year calculated in the income statement is then transferred to the financed by section of the statement of financial position and added to equity.

ASSESSMENT – LET'S CHALLENGE YOUR ACCOUNTING SKILLS

EXERCISE 1

	£
Equity	?
Cash ⎤ (Cash and cash	125
Bank ⎦ equivalents)	6 975
Property	4 000
Motor vehicles	850
Plant and machinery	1 270
Inventory at start Year	21 300
Trade receivables	1 500
Trade payables	800
Sales revenue	18 300
Purchases	6 000
Sales returns	200
Purchase returns	150
Drawings	4 200
Carriage inwards	100
Carriage outwards	150
Wages	1 600
Advertising	1 000
Insurance	500

Final Accounts of a Sole Trader – Assessment Task 1

From the following information taken from the books of M MacAlpine, prepare a trial balance (and determine the equity figure), the income statement for year ended 31 Dec and statement of financial position at that date.

Notes:

Closing inventory end of Year 2: £1000.

Advertising prepaid at 31 December Year 2: £300.

Wages owing £200.

Insurance prepaid at 1 January Year 2 £50 and prepaid at 31 December Year 2: £75.

Depreciate motor vehicles by 5% and plant and machinery by 10%.

EXERCISE 2

	DR	CR
	£	£
Property	115 000	
Fixtures and fittings	18 000	
Provision for depreciation –		
Fixtures and Fittings		1 800
Inventory 1 January Year 2	37 500	
Trade receivables	47 200	
Trade payables		11 300
Cash and cash equivalents	13 000	
Purchases	47 000	
Sales revenue		161 920
Rent and rates	2 500	
Heat and light	,400	
Carriage outwards	500	
Discounts received		2 700
Sales returns	700	
Office salaries	50 000	
Bank loan		20 000
Equity		150 600
Drawings	15 520	
	348 320	348 320

Final Accounts of a Sole Trader – Assessment Task 2

From the following list of balances, prepare the income statement and statement of financial position of R Alburn for the year ended 31 December Year 2:

Notes at 31 December Year 2:

Closing inventory amounted to £39 000.

Office salaries accrued £1600.

Rates prepaid £300.

Interest on loan due £2200.

Fixtures and fittings should be depreciated by a further 10%.

DON'T FORGET

Working notes must be shown. In examinations a wrong figure with no working receives no marks. Figures with workings, showing the correct method, will gain some of the marks.

contd

⚙ EXERCISE 3

	DR	CR
	£	£
Sales revenue		250 000
Net purchases	75 000	
Opening inventory	6 500	
Advertising	800	
Heating and lighting	1 800	
Rent and rates	2 400	
Wages	30 500	
Trade receivables/trade payables	5 400	3 700
Cash and cash equivalents	97 000	
VAT		2 500
Premises	100 000	
Office equipment	25 000	
Plant and machinery	90 000	
Provisions for depreciation –		
Office equipment		5 000
Plant and machinery		30 200
Drawings	6 000	
Equity		149 000
	440 400	440 400

Final Accounts of a Sole Trader – Assessment Task 3

The following information is available for R Gordon, for the year ended 31 October Year 2: Trial balance as at 31 October Year 2

The following additional information is available on 31 October Year 2:

- Closing inventory £5900
- Heating and lighting amount due £200
- Advertising prepaid £200

Further depreciate non-current assets by the following percentages:

- Office equipment 20%
- Plant and machinery 15%

You are required to prepare the income statement for year ended 31 October Year 2 and statement of financial position at that date.

⚙ EXERCISE 4

Final Accounts of a Sole Trader – Assessment Task 4

From the following list of balances of R Trader for the year ended 30 June Year 2, prepare the income statement and statement of financial position at that date taking account of the notes at the end.

	Dr	Cr
	£	£
Purchases and sales revenue	100 000	350 000
Purchase and sales returns	500	200
Opening inventory	10 000	
Carriage outwards	900	
Discount received		500
Insurance	1 850	
Electricity	780	
Office salaries	36 000	
General expenses	24 700	
Trade receivables/trade payables	9 350	4 550
Cash and cash equivalents	6 500	
VAT		3 400
Premises	150 000	
Motor lorries	15 000	
Machinery	120 000	
Provision for depreciation –		
Motor lorries		3 500
Machinery		43 200
Drawings	9 600	
Equity		79 830
	485 180	485 180

Notes to the accounts at 30 June Year 2:

Closing inventory £4900.

General expenses due £300.

Insurance prepaid £400.

Depreciation on non-current assets on the straight line method has to be provided for as follows:

- Motor lorries 25%
- Machinery 15%

DEALING WITH ERRORS IN THE LEDGER ACCOUNTS 1

ERRORS WHICH WILL NOT AFFECT THE TRIAL BALANCE

The rules of double-entry bookkeeping state that:

1. Every debit entry needs a corresponding credit entry;
2. Every credit entry needs a corresponding debit entry.

If these bookkeeping rules are applied consistently, a trial balance can be extracted and the total of all debits will equal the total of all credits, that is it would balance.

Suppose we correctly entered cash sales of £70 to the debit side of the cash account but did not enter the £70 to the credit side of the sales account. If this was the only bookkeeping error, then the trial balance totals would differ by £70. However, there are certain kinds of error which would not affect the agreement of the trial balance totals. These errors are shown here.

ERROR OF COMMISSION

Wrong personal account is used.

EXAMPLE:

On 4 April, Bertie's sold goods on credit to debtor David Black for £60. Although the sales account was credited, the wrong (trade receivable) debtor's account was debited – Martin Black was debited in error. The two accounts affected are David Black and Martin Black.

Sales Revenue A/c

Date	Details	Dr	Cr	Balance
4 April	David Black		60	60

Martin Black A/c

Date	Details	Dr	Cr	Balance
4 April	Sales	60		60
4 April	David Black (correction of error)		60	0

David Black A/c

Date	Details	Dr	Cr	Balance
4 April	Martin Black (correction of error)	60		60

⚙ EXERCISE 1

On 4 April, J Marshall sold goods on credit to debtor Ian McNab for £120. Although the sales account was credited, the wrong debtor's account was debited – Ken McNab was debited in error. The two accounts affected are Ken McNab and Ian McNab.

In your workbook, open up three ledger accounts to show how they would look after the correction of this error of commission.

This will not affect the agreement of the trial balance since there has been both a debit and credit entry.

ERROR OF OMISSION

A transaction has been completely missed out of the ledger accounts.

EXAMPLE:

On 10 April, Kamtec made a payment by cheque to creditor S Wilson for £500. This transaction was completely omitted (missed out) from the ledger. The two accounts affected are bank and S Wilson

Bank Account A/c

Date	Details	Dr	Cr	Balance
10 April	S Wilson (correction of error)		500	500

S Wilson A/c

Date	Details	Dr	Cr	Balance
10 April	Bank (correction of error)	500		500

⚙ EXERCISE 2

On 14 April, S Grant made a payment of £200 to creditor R Young.

This transaction was completely omitted (missed out) from the ledger. The two accounts affected are bank and R Young

In your workbook, open up two ledger accounts to show how they would look after the correction of this error of omission.

This will not affect the agreement of the trial balance since no debit or credit entry has been made.

ERROR OF ORIGINAL ENTRY

Wrong amount entered in both accounts.

EXAMPLE:

On 21 April, Kamtec paid a month's rent by cash £60. This transaction was entered in the correct ledger accounts but recorded as £90 in both accounts instead of £60. The two accounts affected are rent and cash.

Cash A/c

Date	Details	Dr	Cr	Balance
21 April	Rent		90	90
21 April	Rent (correction of error)	30		60

Rent A/c

Date	Details	Dr	Cr	Balance
21 April	Cash	90		90
21 April	Cash (correction of error)		30	60

ERROR OF PRINCIPLE

Transaction entered in the wrong class of account.

EXAMPLE:

On 25 April Kamtec purchased a machine by cheque for £330. This was debited to the purchases account instead of the machinery account.

Bank A/c

Date	Details	Dr	Cr	Balance
25 April	Purchases		330	330

Purchases A/c

Date	Details	Dr	Cr	Balance
25 April	Bank	330		330
25 April	Machine A/c (Correction of error)		330	0

Machine A/c

Date	Details	Dr	Cr	Balance
25 April	Purchases A/c (correction of error)	330		330

COMPENSATING ERROR

One arithmetical error in one account cancels out another arithmetical error in another account.

EXAMPLE:

On 27 April Kamtec discovered that the sales account had been over added by £200, and that the wages account had also been over added by £200.

Sales A/c

Date	Details	Dr	Cr	Balance
27 April	Balance			20 000
27 April	Correction of error – sales over-cast	200		19 800

Wages A/c

Date	Details	Dr	Cr	Balance
27 April	Balance			12 000
27 April	Correction of error – rates over-cast		200	11 800

 **EXERCISE 3**

On 22 April, S Cahill paid one month's insurance by cheque. This transaction was entered in the correct ledger accounts but recorded as £900 in both accounts instead of £90. The two accounts affected are bank and insurance.

In your workbook open up two ledger accounts to show how they would look after the correction of this error of original entry.

This will not affect the agreement of the trial balance since a debit and a credit entry has been made for the same wrong amount in both accounts.

EXERCISE 4

On 26 April L Henderson purchased fixtures and fittings by cash for £200. This was debited to the purchases account instead of the fixtures and fittings account. The three accounts affected are bank, purchases and fixtures and fittings.

In your workbook, open up three ledger accounts to show how they would look after the correction of this error of principle.

This will not affect the agreement of the trial balance since there has been a debit and corresponding credit entry

EXERCISE 5

On 28 April J Kelly notices that purchases have been over added by £100 and that the wages account has also been under added by £100. The two accounts affected are the purchases account and the wages account. These two accounts are shown below prior to the errors being discovered.

Sales A/c

Date	Details	Dr	Cr	Balance
27 April	Balance			10 000
27 April	Correction of error			?

Wages A/c

Date	Details	Dr	Cr	Balance
27 April	Balance			5 000
27 April	Correction of error			?

Show how these would look after the correction of this compensating error.

DEALING WITH ERRORS IN THE LEDGER ACCOUNTS 2

COMPLETE REVERSAL ENTRIES

A debit and a credit is recorded, but the debit is recorded in the account that ought to have been credited and credit is recorded in the account that ought to have been debited. There is still a corresponding debit and credit entry.

EXAMPLE:

On 28 April Kamtec made payment by cheque for £50 to L Donnelly. In error Kamtec debited the bank account and credited L Donnelly. The two accounts affected are bank and L Donnelly.

Bank A/c

Date	Details	Dr	Cr	Balance
28 April	L Donnelly	50		50 (Dr)
28 April	L Donnelly – error complete reversal of entry		100	50 (Cr)

L Donnelly A/c

Date	Details	Dr	Cr	Balance
28 April	Bank		50	50 (Cr)
28 April	Bank – error complete reversal of entry	100		50 (Dr)

 EXERCISE 1

On 29 April R McWhirtter received a cheque for £600 from A Smilie. In error R McWhirtter credited the bank account and debited A Smilie. The two accounts affected are bank and A Smilie.

In your workbook open up these two ledger accounts to show how they would look after the correction of this error of reversal of entry.

This will not affect the agreement of the trial balance since there has been a debit and corresponding credit entry

FURTHER EXERCISES ON DEALING WITH ERRORS IN THE LEDGER ACCOUNTS

 EXERCISE 2

After the final accounts of a sole trader had been drawn up, the following errors were discovered. State the effect that the CORRECTION of each of these errors would have upon the profits. Set out your answer as shown.

Example: Sales over added by £1240

1 Purchases on credit had been over added by £100.

2 Goods valued at £193.50 had been sold on credit to J Gibson but the entry had been debited to the account of J E Gibson.

3 Discount received totalling £55 had been misread as discount allowed and entered accordingly in the final accounts.

4 Closing inventory was originally valued at £6940 and entered in the income statement as that figure. It has since been discovered that it should have been valued at £7000.

Item	Effect upon profit	Amount
Example	Decrease	£1240
1		
2		
3		
4		

 DON'T FORGET

These six errors will not affect the trial balance totals.

ONLINE TEST

Test your knowledge of dealing with errors at www.brightredbooks.net/N5Accounting

 ONLINE

Head online for more tasks about how errors affect the final accounts of a sole trader at www.brightredbooks.net/N5Accounting

contd

EXERCISE 3

Show in the table below, how the following errors would be corrected in the ledger accounts of R Taylor, a sole trader. The first one has been done for you.

1 £18 received from P Park had been posted to the account of D Park.

2 £40 spent by the trader on his own expenses had been posted to the office expenses account.

3 £10 received in respect of the sale of some bookcases from the office had been posted to the sales account.

4 £28 paid to D Allan had been posted to the account of J Callen.

5 £65 spent by R Taylor on office furniture had been posted to the office expenses account.

6 Machinery valued at £1600 purchased on credit from Mitchell Ltd, had been debited to the purchases account.

Error	Account Debited	Amount	Amount Credited	Amount
1	P Park	£18	D Park	£18
2				
3				
4				
5				
6				

EXERCISE 4

Show in the table below, how each of the following errors would be corrected in the ledger accounts of H Gibson. The first one has been done for you.

1 The purchase of a computer, value £750.50, had been wrongly included in the purchases account.

2 A credit note issued to R Morgan for goods returned to the value of £60, less 5% trade discount, had been posted to the account of R Morton.

3 When paying J Johnson, a (trade payable) creditor, Gibson had deducted £5 discount. Johnson had disallowed this discount.

4 A sale to Derby & Co amounting to £275 had been entered in the ledger accounts as £257.

5 Goods sold to K Smith, £89 were not entered into the ledger accounts.

6 A payment made to R Strong, a creditor, of £100 had been entered on the debit side of the cash account and credited in R Strong's account.

Error	Account Debited	Amount	Amount Credited	Amount
1	Machinery account	£750.50	Purchases account	£750.50
2				
3				
4				
5				
6				

THINGS TO DO AND THINK ABOUT

Let's now look and see how errors affect the final accounts of a sole trader.

Copy the following table into your workbook and think about the errors noted in column 1. State, in column 2, whether the correction of the errors will affect the profit for the year. In column 3, state whether the correction will INCREASE, DECREASE or have NO EFFECT on the profit for the year. The first one has been done for you.

Error	Yes/No	Effect on (Profit for the year) Net Profit
Sales over added by £150	Yes	DECREASE
Rent under added by £20		
Rates over added by £50		
Cash payment to a creditor entered in cash account only, £60		
Omission of drawings by cheque £100		
Purchase of machinery £100 entered in ledger accounts as £1000		
Purchases under added by £30		
Purchase of office equipment £50 entered in purchases account only		
Sale of motor van £500 entered in error in sales account		
Advertising under added by £80		
Cash payment by (trade receivable) debtor entered in error on credit side of the cash account		

PREPARING MANAGEMENT ACCOUNTING INFORMATION

BREAK-EVEN ANALYSIS

MANAGEMENT ACCOUNTING: AN INTRODUCTION

In Unit 1 we focused on financial accounting. Financial accounting is concerned mainly with the recording function (called bookkeeping) and the drafting of final accounts of sole traders. The main problem with financial accounting is that it deals with matters which have already happened (so it is really dealing with historic information). You can control what is happening or about to happen, but you cannot change what has already happened!

Management accounting is mainly concerned with the provision of information to enable the management of an organisation to make decisions for the future. Some examples are outlined below:

- Indicating where losses or wastage are occurring and outlining what action should be taken to prevent it happening again.
- Preparing budgets for management to work within and which will ensure good cash flow.
- Deciding if the firm should stop selling or making certain products.
- Controlling the business's stock.
- Working out the cost of jobs to be undertaken to a customer's specific requirements.

DON'T FORGET

Break-even point is when a business does not make a profit or a loss from the making and selling of a product.

BREAK-EVEN ANALYSIS

Break-even analysis is a useful tool to any profit-making business. It may help a business answer some very important questions:

Is producing or selling a certain product going to be profitable?

If no profits are likely to be made from making/selling a product it is unlikely that the business will continue to make/sell the product. Time and resources are likely to be switched into other more profitable products.

How many units of a product would have to be sold before any profit is made?

A business may only produce/sell a certain product if it can do so on a very large scale. Making or selling only a small quantity may prove to be very costly and unprofitable.

What will the profit be at various levels of output?

A business will wish to forecast and plan for the future. As such it will require an indication of profit at various levels of output/sales.

TYPES OF COSTS

Fixed Costs

These are costs that **do not change** with changes in the level of production or sales. Even if no products are made, these costs will still have to be paid. Examples of fixed costs would include rent, insurance and loan interest.

contd

Variable Costs

These are costs that **do change** directly with any changes in production or sales. If no output is made then variable costs will be nil. If output is doubled, so too is this variable cost. Examples of variable costs would include costs of material used to make the product and electricity used to power machines.

Total Costs

Total costs are simply fixed costs and variable costs added together.

TC = FC + VC

As total costs include some of the **variable costs** then total costs will also change with any changes in output/sales. For example, if output/sales rise then so too will total costs. If output/sales fall, then total costs will also fall.

Let's look at an example:

EXAMPLE

Lee Henderson, makes and sells chocolate bars.
He has **fixed costs** of £600 per annum.

Variable costs of making each chocolate bar include:

Materials – 60p per unit ⎫
Electricity – 15p per unit ⎬ 75p

Lee Henderson **sells** each unit of output (chocolate bar) for £1 each.

The table below calculates the profit or loss at each of the various levels of output shown.

Output	Sales Revenue	Fixed Costs	Variable Costs	Total Costs	Profit/Loss
	Output x £1		Output x 75p	FC+VC	SR-TC
0	£0	£600	£0	£600	(£600) Loss
400	£400	£600	£300	£900	(£500) Loss
800	£800	£600	£600	£1200	(£400) Loss
1200	£1200	£600	£900	£1500	(£300) Loss
1600	£1600	£600	£1200	£1800	(£200) Loss
2000	£2000	£600	£1500	£2100	(£100) Loss
2400	£2400	£600	£1800	£2400	No profit or loss
2800	£2800	£600	£2100	£2700	£100 profit
3200	£3200	£600	£2400	£3000	£200 profit

ONLINE

Watch the clip at www.brightredbooks.net/N5Accounting to see an explanation of the break-even point!

THINGS TO DO AND THINK ABOUT

Look again at the example above, then answer the following questions.

1. At what level of output does Lee Henderson not make a profit or a loss?
2. What is this level of output called?
3. At what level of output does the business first make a profit?
4. What is the business incurring below break-even point, that is when it is making an output of 2000 units or less?

ONLINE TEST

Test your knowledge of break-even analysis at www.brightredbooks.net/N5Accounting

BREAK-EVEN CHARTS

Sales, fixed costs, total costs and break-even (B/E) point can be shown on a graph.

STEPS FOR PREPARING A B/E CHART

1. All charts should have a suitable heading.
2. Costs and revenue are shown on the vertical axis.
3. Output is shown on the horizontal axis.
4. Total revenue should be plotted first – plot the lowest possible total revenue first. Then plot the highest possible total revenue. Join the two points together using a ruler and label TR.
5. Plot total costs next – plot the lowest possible total costs first. Then plot the highest possible total costs. Join the two points together using a ruler and label TC.
6. Indicate B/E point where both lines cross.
7. Indicate the area of loss below the B/E point.
8. Indicate the area of profit above B/E point.

ADVANTAGES OF USING GRAPHS

- Easily understood as it compares costs to sales.
- Highlights area of profit and area of loss.
- Can calculate profit and loss at various levels of output.
- Easy to show margin of safety.
- Can forecast profit and different levels of output.
- Visual impact – B/E point quickly and easily seen.

⚙ EXERCISE 1

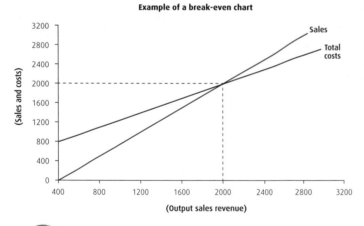

Example of a break-even chart

Study the graph and answer these questions.

1. At what level of output does the business break-even?
2. What is the sales revenue at this level of output?
3. From the graph, identify fixed costs.
4. Copy the graph onto graph paper and shade in the area of profit one colour and the area of loss another colour.

⚙ EXERCISE 2

The following figures have been supplied by A Crockery, who is considering setting up in business as a sole trader, making and selling plates. He is particularly concerned to know how many plates he must make and sell before the product becomes profitable.

Fixed costs = £1000
Variable costs per plate = £3
Selling price per plate = £8

(a) Copy and complete the table using the information above. The first row has been completed for you.
(b) At what level of output does A Crockery break even?
(c) Plot fixed costs, total costs and sales revenue on a sheet of graph paper. Plot output on the vertical axis and costs on the vertical axis.
(d) Indicate the break-even point and shade in the area of profit and the area of loss using two different colours.

Units of Output	Fixed Costs	Variable Costs	Total Costs	Sales Revenue	Profit/ (Loss)
	FC	VC	FC+VC		
0	£1000	–	£1000	–	£1000 (Loss)
100					
200					
300					
400					
500					

EXERCISE 3

(a) Copy and complete the table and calculate total costs from the information shown.

(b) On a sheet of graph paper, construct a break-even chart. You should plot costs and total revenue on the vertical axis and output on the horizontal axis.

(c) Identify the number of units at which the firm breaks even.

(d) On your completed graph, shade in the area of profit and the area of loss using two different colours.

Units	Fixed Costs	Variable Costs	Total Costs	Total Revenue (Sales)
0	£3 000	–	£3 000	–
1000	£3 000	£2 000		£3 000
2000	£3 000	£4 000		£6 000
3000	£3 000	£6 000		£9 000
4000	£3 000	£8 000		£12 000
5000	£3 000	£10 000		£15 000

EXERCISE 4

J Craig sells equipment to the farm industry. His fixed costs are £10 000 and each machine costs him £400 to buy. He sells them for £600 each and is trying to work out his profit or loss at various levels of sales. He has worked out the following:

(a) You should copy the table above and complete the total costs and profit/loss columns.

(b) Using the information in the table, construct a break-even chart on a sheet of graph paper. You should plot total costs and sales revenue on the vertical axis and output on the horizontal axis.

(c) When you have completed your graph you should show break-even point in units and sales value, area of profit and areas of loss.

Units Sold	Fixed Costs	Variable Costs	Total Costs	Sales	Profit/Loss
0	£10 000	–		–	
10	£10 000	£4 000		£6 000	
20	£10 000	£8 000		£12 000	
30	£10 000	£12 000		£18 000	
40	£10 000	£16 000		£24 000	
50	£10 000	£20 000		£30 000	
60	£10 000	£24 000		£36 000	
70	£10 000	£28 000		£42 000	
80	£10 000	£32 000		£48 000	
90	£10 000	£36 000		£54 000	
100	£10 000	£40 000		£60 000	

CALCULATION OF BREAK-EVEN POINT USING A FORMULA

$$\text{Break-even (B/E)} = \frac{\text{Fixed costs (FC)}}{\text{Contribution per unit (C)}}$$

Contribution (C) = Selling price per unit (SP) – Variable cost per unit (VC)

EXAMPLE:

Fixed costs = £600
Selling price per unit = £50
Variable cost per unit = £20
Contribution = £50–£20 = £30
This means that every unit sold is 'contributing' £30 towards paying fixed costs.
How many units would then have to be sold to cover fixed costs?

$$\text{Break-even} = \frac{\text{Fixed costs}}{\text{Contribution}} = \frac{£600}{£30}$$

= 20 units

When the 20th unit is sold the firm breaks-even, that is it does not make a profit or a loss. In other words, **sales revenue** exactly equals **total cost**.

When the 21st unit is sold this **contributes** £30 towards the business's profits.

ONLINE

Try out some more exercises on break-even charts at www.brightredbooks.net/N5Accounting

DON'T FORGET

Contribution per unit goes towards paying fixed costs – once ALL fixed costs have been paid, contribution goes towards profit.

THINGS TO DO AND THINK ABOUT

PROGRESS CHECK

Answer the following questions:

1. Explain, using an example, what is meant by fixed costs.
2. Outline how total costs are calculated.
3. Explain, using an example, what is meant by variable costs.
4. Outline two advantages of using a chart to show break-even point.
5. State the terms used to describe the point at which a business does not make a profit or a loss.

ONLINE TEST

Test your knowledge of break-even charts at www.brightredbooks.net/N5Accounting

EXERCISES ON BREAK-EVEN CHARTS

⚙ EXERCISE 1

A firm has fixed costs of £1200. The selling price for its product is £6 per unit and the variable cost is £3 per unit.

Using this information, copy and complete the table below.

State the level of production where break-even point is achieved.

Units	Fixed Costs	Variable Costs	Total Costs	Sales Revenue	Profit/Loss
0					
200					
400					
600					
800					
1000					

⚙ EXERCISE 3

The following table shows costs and revenues at various levels of output.

Copy and complete the table below then calculate the missing figures indicated by letters A–I.

No. of Putters Produced	Fixed Costs	Variable Costs	Total Costs	Revenue
0	£1200	0	A	0
100	B	£2500	C	£3000
200	£1200	D	£6200	£6000
300	£1200	£7500	£8700	E
400	F	G	H	I

⚙ EXERCISE 2

The following table shows the costs and revenues at various levels of output.

Copy and complete the table below then calculate the missing figures indicated by letters A–I.

Units	Fixed Costs	Variable Costs	Total Costs	Revenue
0	£600	0	A	0
100	B	£150	C	£400
200	£600	D	£900	£800
300	£600	£450	£1050	E
400	F	G	H	I

⚙ EXERCISE 4

Use the information in the following table to prepare a break-even chart on a sheet of graph paper.

Total costs and revenue should be plotted on the vertical axis and units/output on the horizontal axis.

The number of units required to break-even should be clearly indicated. You should also shade the area of profit and the area of loss using two different colours.

Units	Fixed Costs	Variable Costs	Total Costs	Revenue
0	600	0	600	0
100	600	200	800	400
200	600	400	1000	800
300	600	600	1200	1200
400	600	800	1400	1600
500	600	1000	1600	2000

⚙ EXERCISE 5

Irene Barbour decides to rent a stall at her local market for 1 year with the purpose of selling candy floss. She has worked out her costs as follows:

Fixed costs

Stall rental	£300
Wages of assistant	£900
Advertising	£10
Electricity	£40
	£1250

Variable cost per tub of candy floss = 40p

Selling price per tub of candy floss = 50p

Copy and complete a break-even table with the following headings and the following sales possibilities:

Units Sold	Fixed Costs	Variable Costs	Total Costs	Sales	Profit or Loss
0					
2500					
5000					
7500					
10000					
12500					
15000					
17500					
20000					

Using the figures from the table above, draw up a break-even chart on suitable graph paper.

You should plot total costs and sales on the vertical axis and output on the horizontal axis.

On the chart you should clearly indicate the break-even point.

You should also shade in the area of loss and the area of profit on the graph using two different colours.

CONTRIBUTION

Contribution is the term used to describe the difference between selling price (SP) per unit and variable cost (VC) per unit. Contribution IS NOT profit. Contribution per unit goes towards paying fixed costs. Once fixed costs have been paid in full, any further contribution will go towards profit.

EXAMPLE 1

From the information below, calculate contribution per unit.

Selling price per unit =	**£1.00**
Variable cost per unit =	**£0.75**
Contribution per unit =	

EXAMPLE 2

From the information below, calculate contribution per unit.

Selling price per unit =	**£4.00**
Variable cost per unit =	**£2.50**
Contribution per unit =	

EXAMPLE 3

From the information below, calculate contribution per unit.

Selling price per unit =	**£6.50**
Variable cost per unit =	**£1.25**
Contribution per unit =	

EXERCISE 6

Jean MacKinnon owns and runs a business that manufactures and sells handbags. In 2016, she plans to produce and sell 500 handbags at £45 each.
She estimates the following costs:
Administration £2500, Rent £2000, Heat & Light £1500

The production costs for each handbag are:
Labour £12, Materials £13

(a) Using the information above, copy and complete the break-even statement below to calculate how many handbags would have to be produced and sold to allow Jean to break-even.

ESTIMATED BREAK-EVEN STATEMENT OF JEAN MACKINNON FOR THE YEAR ENDED 31 DECEMBER 2016		
	£	£
Sales (revenue per handbag)		
LESS UNIT VARIABLE COSTS		
Labour		
Materials		
CONTRIBUTION (RETURN)		
PER UNIT HANDBAG		
Break-even point = $\dfrac{\text{Fixed cost}}{\text{Contribution per unit}}$ = ___ = ___ units		

(b) Calculate the profit or loss if 400 handbags are produced and sold in 2016.
(c) State two advantages of using a break-even chart.

EXERCISE 7

From the information below, prepare a break-even chart to show fixed costs, total costs and sales revenue lines. Indicate the break-even point on your diagram.

Variable costs per unit:
Materials £10, Labour £15 (total variable cost per unit = £25)
Selling price per unit = £40
Total fixed costs = £60 000
Projected output levels 1000 units – 8000 units.
Before plotting your break-even chart, copy and complete the table below.

Output	Sales Revenue	Variable Cost	Total Contribution	Fixed Costs	Profit/Loss
0	0	0	0	£60 000	£60 000 loss
1000	£40 000	£25 000	£15 000	£60 000	£45 000 loss
2000					
3000					
4000					
5000					
6000					
7000					
8000					

Now use the table to plot your graph.
From the chart find the break-even point in:

- units of output
- sales value

Shade the area of profit and the area of loss on your chart using two different colours. Find the profit expected at outputs of 6000 units and 8000 units.
Management are considering increasing the selling price to £45 per unit. Calculate the new levels of sales revenue at the different levels of output. Add this new sales line to your chart and clearly show the **new break-even point**.
State the new break-even point in

- units of output
- sales value

Find the expected profit at outputs of 4000 and 6000 units.

ONLINE

Try out some more exercises on break-even charts at www.brightredbooks.net/N5Accounting

ONLINE TEST

Test your knowledge of break-even charts at www.brightredbooks.net/N5Accounting

THINGS TO DO AND THINK ABOUT

Work alone or with a partner and write a definition of these keywords:

Fixed costs	Total costs	Contribution
Variable costs	Break-even	Total Revenue

MARGIN OF SAFETY (MOS)

WHAT IS THE MARGIN OF SAFETY?

Margin of safety (MOS) is the term used to describe the difference between:

1. Sales revenue at break-even point and **actual** sales revenue;
2. Units of output at break-even point and **actual** units of output.

⚙ EXERCISE 1

Copy and complete the table below and then calculate the margin of safety in units of output for each of the following businesses. The first one has been done for you.

NAME OF BUSINESS	UNITS OF OUTPUT TO BREAK-EVEN	CURRENT LEVEL OF OUTPUT IN UNITS	MARGIN OF SAFETY (MOS)
Firm A	500 units	2000 units	1500 units
Firm B	800 units	900 units	
Firm C	2000 units	3250 units	
Firm D	550 units	2400 units	
Firm E	600 units	650 units	

⚙ EXERCISE 2

Copy and complete the table below and then calculate the margin of safety in sales revenue for each of the following businesses. The first one has been done for you.

NAME OF BUSINESS	SALES REVENUE TO BREAK-EVEN	CURRENT LEVEL OF SALES REVENUE	MARGIN OF SAFETY (MOS)
Firm A	£15 000	£25 000	£10 000
Firm B	£22 000	£70 000	
Firm C	£45 000	£90 000	
Firm D	£60 000	£70 000	
Firm E	£150 000	£600 000	

⚙ EXERCISE 3

(a) Calculate the break-even point in units from the following information
   Variable cost per unit £0.20
   Fixed costs £2000
   Selling price per unit £0.40
(b) What is the margin of safety in units if 15 000 units are currently being produced?

⚙ EXERCISE 4

(a) Calculate the break-even point in units from the following information
   Variable cost per unit £5.00
   Fixed costs £15 000
   Selling price per unit £10
(b) What is the margin of safety in units if 3000 units are currently being produced?

⚙ EXERCISE 5

A factory produces hedge clippers at a variable cost of £5 each.
The annual total fixed costs of the factory are £10 000.
The clippers sell to wholesalers at £8 each.

(a) How many clippers need to be produced before a profit is made?
(b) Calculate the total profit made at full production of 6000 units.
(c) Calculate the change in total profit at full production if:
   (i)   the price of materials is increased by 20%
   (ii) the selling price increases or decreases by 25%
   (iii) the rent increases or decreases by 10%.

 ONLINE

Try out some more exercises on margins of safety at www.brightredbooks.net/N5Accounting

⚙ EXERCISE 6

You are given the following information
for a business which manufactures shoes.

From the information shown, you are required to calculate:
(a) Break-even point in units and sales value
(b) Sales level required to make a profit of:
   (i)   £432 000   (ii)   £108 000
(c) Profit or loss made at the following sales levels:
   (i)   18 000 units   (ii)   800 units
(d) Margin of safety in sales value and units at the current
   level of output of 14 000 units.

Fixed costs per month	£27 000
Variable costs per unit:	
Materials	£34
Direct labour	£12
Variable overheads	£34
Selling price per unit	£100

⚙ EXERCISE 7

You are given the following information
for a business which manufactures armchairs.

From the information shown, you are required to calculate:
(a) Break-even point in units and sales value
(b) Sales level required to make a profit of:
   (i)   £648 000   (ii)   £162 000
(c) Profit or loss made at the following sales levels:
   (i)   27 000 units   (ii)   600 units
(d) Margin of safety in sales value and units at the current
   level of output of 21 000 units.

Fixed Costs per month	£40 500
Variable costs per unit:	
Materials	£51
Direct Labour	£18
Variable Overheads	£51
Selling Price per unit	£300

⚠ THINGS TO DO AND THINK ABOUT

PROGRESS CHECK

Answer the following questions in your workbook.

1. Explain, using an example, what is meant by the term contribution.
2. Describe what is meant by margin of safety.
3. State the two ways in which the margin of safety can be expressed.
4. State the terms used to describe the areas above and below break-even point on a
   break-even chart.

 ONLINE TEST

Test your knowledge of margins of safety at www.brightredbooks.net/N5Accounting

INVENTORY VALUATION 1

VALUING INVENTORY

An important part of inventory control is the recording of inventory movements within a business. Valuing inventory might at first seem to be a simple enough exercise but this is not the case for the reason that there are several alternative methods of valuation, each producing a different figure. We will consider two of these methods later in this unit. The value placed on a business's inventory is of crucial importance, because:

1. it will affect the materials to be charged to customers for completing jobs;
2. it affects the figure for cost of sales sold which in turn will affect the gross profit in the income statement – see Unit 1;
3. it affects the value of current assets in a business's statement of financial position – see Unit 1.

TYPES OF (INVENTORY) STOCK CONTROL SYSTEMS

Inventory Record Cards

Inventory record cards contain, in addition to the quantities of receipts and issues of inventory, a record of the prices of inventory received and issued. It may also include data on the level at which inventory should be re-ordered and in what quantities.

Computers

The recording of inventory movements is frequently done today by means of computer (using an Excel spreadsheet). The great advantage of using a computer for inventory control is that accurate details can be supplied to management much more quickly and accurately.

Inventory card

| Stock Item: | Woollen Jumpers | | | | | | | Location: | Aisle 16 | |
| Stock Code: | WJ | | | | | | | Supplier: | Merino Mills | |

| | | IN | | | OUT | | | BALANCE | | |
Date	Details	Qty	Unit cost	Value	Qty	Unit cost	Value	Qty	Unit cost	Value
July 1	Balance							8	30	240
2	Inv. 49				6	30	180	2	30	60
3	Ch. 142	12	35	420				2	30	60
								12	35	420
9	Rec. 23				2	30	60			
					8	35	280	4	35	140

STORAGE AND LOCATION OF INVENTORY

In choosing the location for stores, the factors which have to be considered are:

- the type of production process and the inventory involved, e.g. is the inventory bulky and difficult to move from one location to another?
- the nature of materials, e.g. are they flammable? If so, the stores may have to be located in a more isolated area.
- the time taken to transport materials from the stores to the production areas.

The type of storage used for materials will depend upon:

- the **weight** of the goods
- the **bulkiness** of the goods
- the risk of physical **deterioration**
- the risk of **theft**.

INVENTORY CHECKING/TAKING

The physical checking of inventory is necessary for the following reasons:

- to ensure inventory records are accurate
- to act as a deterrent against theft
- to detect errors and discrepancies and therefore update inventory record cards.

METHODS OF CHECKING INVENTORY

Checking Inventory Periodically

Checking inventory periodically is usually undertaken annually (once per year) and is done by physically counting inventory on shelves, including any work in progress.

Checking Inventory on a Continuous Basis

Checking inventory on a continuous basis is essential where an organisation uses what is known as the **perpetual inventory system.** This is a stocktaking system whereby the inventory balance is shown on the inventory record card after every receipt or issue of stock. If the inventory record cards are to be relied upon, any differences between the balances on the inventory record card and the actual inventory levels must be investigated immediately.

The differences may arise due to errors completing inventory stock cards, shrinkage of materials, theft and losses due to damages.

INVENTORY LEVELS

There are disadvantages of having too much or too little inventory.

Disadvantages of Holding Too Much Inventory

- high storage costs
- cash being paid to purchase inventory before it is absolutely necessary
- high risk of deterioration or obsolescence before it is able to be used in production.

Disadvantages of Not Holding Enough Inventory

- running out of inventory and so holding up production
- customers going elsewhere if production is halted due to insufficient inventory
- purchasing inventory regularly in small quantities may mean the business does not qualify for trade discounts.

Therefore, it is important that the management accountants ensure that the business has just the right amount of inventory – they must have an efficient inventory control system. Any good inventory control system should pay attention to the following:

- maximum inventory level
- minimum inventory level
- reorder inventory level
- reorder quantity.

MAXIMUM INVENTORY LEVEL	MINIMUM INVENTORY LEVEL
The level which inventory should not rise above. Consider the following: · the cost of storage · the rate of usage · the risk of deterioration.	The minimum inventory level is the level below which inventory should not fall. Consider the following: · the rate of usage · delivery time for new inventory to arrive · the level of safety or 'buffer' or 'safety' inventory to be held.
REORDER LEVEL OF INVENTORY	REORDER QUANTITY
This is the level at which a purchase order is made out. Consider the following: · rate of inventory usage · level of buffer or safety inventory required · the cost of storage.	This is the quantity of materials to be ordered when the reorder level is reached and it depends upon the: · cost of ordering the inventory, for example delivery costs · cost of storing the inventory · trade discounts for bulk buying.

ONLINE

Learn more about inventory control by following the link at www.brightredbooks.net/N5Accounting

 THINGS TO DO AND THINK ABOUT

PROGRESS CHECK

Answer the following questions in your workbook.

1. Outline the factors that should be considered when deciding where to locate the stores department within a business.
2. Explain what is meant by periodic inventory control.
3. Explain what is meant by the perpetual inventory system of stock control.
4. Outline the main disadvantages to a business of not holding enough inventory.
5. Outline the main disadvantages to a business of holding too much inventory.

ONLINE TEST

Test your knowledge of inventory control at www.brightredbooks.net/N5Accounting

INVENTORY VALUATION 2

There are two main methods of valuing inventory:

1. First In First Out (FIFO)   2. Last In First Out (LIFO)

FIRST IN FIRST OUT (FIFO)

The First In First Out (FIFO) method of issuing inventory is based on the first inventory received being the first inventory issued to customers or to production. Issues of inventory will be charged at the first price paid for inventory until all the inventory at that price is used up. Then the next price will be used until all the inventories from that receipt (batch) are used up and so on.

EXAMPLE

Bought		£	Sold		£
January	10 units @ £30 each	300	May	8 @ £50 each	400
April	10 units @ £34 each	340	November	24 @ £60 each	1440
October	20 units @ £40 each	800			
		1440			1840

Date	Received	Issued	Total Balance
January	10 @ £30 = £300		10 @ £30 = £300
April	10 @ £34 = £340		10 @ £30 = £300 10 @ £34 = £340
May		8 @ £30 = £240	2 @ £30 = £60 10 @ £34 = £340
October	20 @ £40 = £800		2 @ £30 = £60 10 @ £34 = £340 20 @ £40 = £800
November		2 @ £30 = £60 10 @ £34 = £340 12 @ £40 = £480	**8 @ £40 = £320**

The total value of closing inventory using the FIFO method is £320.

Advantages of using FIFO for Inventory Valuation

1. It is a logical method because normally goods would be issued in the same order as they are purchased. (Especially perishable products like food).
2. It is an easy system to operate.
3. The balance of inventory is always a true and fair valuation of the business's inventory as it is the most recent inventory purchased that is left.

Disadvantages of using FIFO for Inventory Valuation

1. Clerical errors may be made because of having to select inventory from different batches.
2. It is difficult to compare prices of jobs charged to customers as inventory for one job is likely to be taken from more than one batch. Different prices may be quoted to customers for the same job where inventory is taken from different batches.
3. When inventory prices are increasing, the charge to production will be low (because we may have bought the first batch quite a long time ago and therefore the price would have been low), but the replacement cost will be much higher because prices will have risen since the earlier inventory was purchased.

LAST IN FIRST OUT (LIFO)

The Last In First Out (LIFO) method of valuing inventory is based on the last inventory received being the first inventory issued to customers or production. Issues of inventory will be charged at the last price paid for inventory until all the inventory at that price is used up. Then the next price will be used until all the inventories from that receipt (batch) are used up and so on.

contd

EXAMPLE

Bought	£	Sold	£
January 10 units @ £30 each	300	May 8 @ £50 each	400
April 10 units @ £34 each	340	November 24 @ £60 each	1440
October 20 units @ £40 each	800		
	1440		1840

Date	Received	Issued	Balance
January	10 @ £30 = £300		10 @ £30 = £300
April	10 @ £24 = £240		10 @ £30 = £300
			10 @ £34 = £340
May		8 @ £34 = £272	10 @ £30 = £300
			2 @ £34 = £68
October	20 @ £40 = £800		10 @ £30 = £300
			2 @ £34 = £68
			20 @ £40 = £800
November		20 @ £40 = £800	**8 @ £30 = £240**
		2 @ £34 = £68	
		2 @ £30 = £60	

The total value of closing inventory using the LIFO method is £240.

STOCK VALUATION AND SPREADSHEETS

Excel spreadsheets can be used to value stock. Simple formulae can be used to instantly calculate totals or balances. Spreadsheets also make it easy to make changes to inventory records, save your work and print it out as and when required. See the simple example shown below.

EXAMPLE

	A	B	C	D	E	F
1	INVENTORY VALUATION					
2	DATE	RECEIPTS		ISSUES		BALANCE
3	January	10 @ £50	£500			=C3-E3
4	February			5 @ £50	£250	=F3+C4-E4
5	March	10 @ £25	£250			=F4+C5-E5
6						
7						
8						

Advantages of using LIFO for Inventory Valuation

1. Inventory is issued to jobs or customers at the most up-to-date prices.
2. The cost of inventory being issued is nearly always close to current market value and replacement costs.

Disadvantages of using LIFO for Inventory Valuation

1. The inventory balance which results from this method is based on the oldest stocks and therefore will be out-of-date (i.e. will not be the same as current prices).
2. Clerical errors may be made because of having to select inventory from different batches.
3. A comparison of different jobs may be misleading. If two jobs are carried out one after the other, it may be that the cost of issues to the second job is less than those issued to the first job. This may happen if the issues for the second job are deemed to come from the previous cheaper batch of purchases.
4. There is a high risk of inventory deteriorating if the last inventory in is the first inventory issued to customers or production.

DON'T FORGET

There are advantages and disadvantages of both the FIFO and LIFO systems; business owners and sole traders will consider all of these before deciding which method to use for their business.

ONLINE

Learn more about inventory valuation by completing the exercises at www. brightredbooks.net/ N5Accounting

ONLINE TEST

Test your knowledge of inventory valuation at www.brightredbooks.net/ N5Accounting

THINGS TO DO AND THINK ABOUT

PROGRESS CHECK

Answer the following questions in your workbook.

1. State the factors that should be considered when setting maximum and minimum inventory levels.
2. Explain how the FIFO system issues and values inventory to be charged to a job.
3. Outline one advantage and one disadvantage of using the FIFO method of issuing inventory.
4. Explain how the LIFO system issues and values inventory to be charged to a job.
5. Outline one advantage and one disadvantage of using the LIFO method of issuing inventory.
6. Explain the difference between re-order inventory level and re-order inventory quantity.

EXERCISES ON LIFO AND FIFO

 **EXERCISE 1**

From the following information prepare the inventory ledger card for material Beta using the FIFO method of valuing inventory issues:

March 1 Balance 1,200 units at £1.50
March 4 Receipts 2,000 units at £1.55
March 5 Issued 2,000 units to Job 56A
March 18 Receipts 1,000 units at £1.60
March 20 Issued another 20 units to Job 56A
March 21 Issued 1,200 units to Job 57A

Material Beta

Date	Received	Issued	Balance

 **EXERCISE 2**

From the following information prepare and complete the inventory record card for material Alpha using the LIFO method of valuing inventory issues:

April 1 Balance 200 units at £10
April 4 Receipts 500 units at £10.50
April 5 Issued 300 units to Job 125
April 18 Receipts 100 units at £11
April 20 Returned 25 of the units purchased on 18 April (wrong specification)
April 21 Issued 250 units to Job 126

Material Alpha

Date	Received	Issued	Balance

You should now complete the remaining exercises manually on inventory stock cards/A4 paper or using an Excel spreadsheet.

EXERCISE 3

Use the following information to complete the inventory ledger card for Material Axa for the first week of January. The firm uses the FIFO method of inventory valuation.

January 1 Balance of inventory held in the warehouse amounted to 1,000 units at a cost of 50p per unit
January 3 Issued to production 500 units
January 4 Received into inventory 500 units costing 60p each
January 5 Issued 600 units to production
January 6 Received into inventory 500 units costing 65p
January 7 Returned 200 units received on 6 January (damaged in transit)
January 7 Issued to production 600 units

EXERCISE 4

Complete the stores ledger card for new material Zetta for the following transactions. The firm uses the FIFO method of inventory pricing.

April 1 400 units purchased at £1.00
April 2 100 units issued to Job S123
April 3 10 units purchased on April 1 returned (wrong colour)
April 8 190 units purchased at £1.30
April 20 400 units issued to Job S124
May 6 20 units issued to Job S123
May 9 300 units purchased at £1.20
May 27 500 units purchased at £1.10
May 28 5 units purchased on May 27 returned to supplier (faulty)
May 28 300 units issued to Job S125

EXERCISE 5

From the following information prepare the inventory ledger card for material Gilo using the LIFO method of valuing inventory issues:

Apr-01	Balance 600 units at £2
Apr-04	Receipts 1,000 units at £2.20
Apr-05	Issued 1,200 units to Job 56A
Apr-18	Receipts 500 units at £2.25
Apr-20	Returned 100 of the units purchased on 18 April (damaged)
Apr-21	Issued 600 units to Job 57A

cont

⚙ EXERCISE 6

From the following information prepare and complete the inventory record card for material Beta using the LIFO method of valuing inventory issues:

Jul-01	Balance 400 units at £20
Jul-04	Receipts 1,000 units at £21
Jul-05	Issued 600 units to Job 125
Jul-18	Receipts 100 units at £22
Jul-20	Returned 20 of the units purchased on 18 July (wrong specification)
Jul-21	Issued 500 units to Job 126

⚙ EXERCISE 7

Use the following information to complete the inventory ledger card for Material Gamma for the first week of January. The firm uses the LIFO method of inventory valuation.

Jan-01	Balance of inventory held in the warehouse amounted 20,000 units at a cost of 50p per unit
Jan-04	Issued to production 10,000 units
Jan-08	Received into inventory 10,000 units costing 60p each
Jan-09	Issued 2,000 units to production
Jan-10	Received into inventory 5,000 units costing 65p each
Jan-11	Returned 1,000 of the units received on 8 January (damaged in transit)
Jan-17	Issued to production 6,000 units

⚙ EXERCISE 8

Complete the stores ledger card for new material Xena for the following transactions. The firm uses the LIFO method of inventory pricing.

Feb-01	10,000 units purchased at £1.00
Feb-02	5,000 units issued to Batch 1
Feb-03	1,000 units purchase on February 1 returned (wrong specification)
Feb-08	5,000 units purchased at £1.30
Feb-20	4,000 units issued to Batch 2
Mar-06	2,000 units issued to Batch 3
Mar-09	3,000 units purchased at £1.20
Mar-27	5,000 units purchased at £1.10
Mar-28	500 units purchased on March 27 to supplier (wrong specification)
Mar-28	3,000 units issued to Batch 4

⚙ EXERCISE 9

Receipts		Sales	
Jan	20 at £30 each	Jun	6 for £45 each
May	10 at £33 each	Aug	22 for £46 each
Jul	16 at £38.50 each	Dec	10 for £48 each
Oct	12 at £39 each		

There was no opening inventory in trade. You are required to calculate the closing inventory-in-trade using FIFO and LIFO.

⚙ EXERCISE 10

The following information relates to purchases and issues of an item of inventory which was added to the inventory list as from January 1:

Date	Ref	Details
Jan-14	2078	Purchased 400 at £15.00 each
Feb-09	2123	Purchased 100 at £15.75 each
Mar-11	2208	Purchased 200 at £17.50 each
Mar-14	9764	Issued 320
Apr-27	2389	Purchased 200 at £16.50 each
May-14	9945	Issued 320

You are required to write up the inventory ledger card for the above item using:

1. FIFO method
2. LIFO method

⚙ EXERCISE 11

The following receipts and issues were made in respect of Swivel Pins manufactured on the premises and held in inventory for future use in the Assembly Department.

Swivel Pin 70492/3

Date	Receipts	Date	Issues
Jan-11	50 at £3.72 each	Feb-09	40
Jan-23	20 at £4.35 each	Feb-18	40
Feb-07	100 at £3.39 each		
Feb-14	20 at £5.40 each		
Feb-22	5 at £4.53 each		

Prepare stores ledger cards to show these transactions and the balance in hand. Two records cards are required, showing material requisitions priced on the basis of FIFO and LIFO.

ONLINE

For more exercises on inventory valuation, head to www.brightredbooks.net

LABOUR REMUNERATION

Labour can be one of the biggest costs that a business faces. It is important that careful control is kept of all labour costs or in other words, wages. There are two main reasons why:

1. Labour cost is a major portion of the total cost of making a product for a business to sell, or completing a job for a customer.

2. Labour cost is more difficult to control than material cost due to the human element involved.

In this unit, we will look at the different ways of recording and calculating labour remuneration.

METHODS OF REMUNERATION – (PAYMENT OF WAGES)

Time-Based Systems

In time-based systems payment is made by the hour, week or month irrespective of the level of output or how hard the employee works. This method is used when:

- it is difficult to measure output per worker;
- all workers are doing the same type of work;
- quality rather than quantity of work is required.

EXAMPLE

Employees work a 35-hour week for which they are paid £10 per hour. Earnings are calculated as follows:

Earnings = Hours worked x Rate per Hour = 35 hours x £10 = £350

Advantages of Time-Based Systems:

- it is easy to calculate wages, with no need to refer to output;
- easy to understand for both employee and employer;
- wage costs can be predicted fairly accurately;
- suitable system for calculating wages in a situation where output cannot be measured.

Disadvantages of Time-Based Systems:

- this system does not provide an incentive for workers to work harder;
- wages have to be paid to workers even if no work is available for workers to do;
- workers suffer from low morale as there is no reward for working hard or increasing output;
- management must accurately record the time worked by each employee.

Overtime

The overtime rate is an extra amount paid for each hour worked over the basic working week. The amount of overtime pay will depend on when the extra hours are worked. It is usual for overtime worked on a Saturday and Sunday to be paid at a higher rate than if worked on a weekday.

EXAMPLE

In a firm the basic hours worked are 38 hours per week. Workers are paid a basic rate of £9 per hour.

In the first week on September, S Singh worked 47 hours. The overtime hours were made up as follows:

- 4 hours on a Sunday – this is paid at double time (£9+£9= £18)
- 3 hours on a Saturday – this is paid at time and a half (£9+£4.50= £13.50)
- 2 hours during the week – this is paid at time and a third (£9+£3=£12)

The amount earned by S Singh would be as follows:

Employee – S Singh		
Basic rate	38 hours x £9	£342.00
Week day overtime	2 hours x £12	£24.00
Saturday overtime	3 hours x £13.50	£40.50
Sunday overtime	4 hours x £18	£72.00
TOTAL WAGE DUE TO BE PAID		£478.50

contd

Straight Piece-Work/Rate

In the piece-work system, the employer pays a specified amount for each unit produced. The wage earned by the employee depends on the amount of work carried out during the week. This method of paying wages is suitable for production when large quantities of an identical product are produced.

EXAMPLE

Workers in the Production Department are paid 15p per unit produced.

J Mitchell (Employee Number EN341) produces 1250 units in Week 10. His wage for that week will be calculated as follows:

Wage = No. of units produced x 15p = 1250 x 15p = £187.50

Advantages of Piece-Work Systems:

- simple to operate and calculate;
- incentive for workers to work hard and increase output;
- good system when simple and identical units are being produced.

Disadvantages of Piece-Work Systems:

- all units require to be checked to ensure high quality;
- workers' wages can fluctuate from week to week;
- workers may sacrifice quality for quantity of output to increase wages;
- workers become bored with repetitive and routine work.

Bonus Schemes

With time-based payments, any increase in production levels benefits the employer. On the other hand with piece-rate payments, any increase in production levels benefits the employee. Bonus schemes share the benefits of increased production levels between the employer and employee.

EXAMPLE

It is estimated that it will take 15 hours to paint the games hall in a school. The painter will be paid £10 per hour. A bonus of one third of the time saved × the time rate will be paid.

If the painter completes the work in the 15 hours his wage will be:

Number of hours × Hourly rate =
15 hours × £10 = £150

If the painter completes the job in 12 hours (saving 3 hours) his wage will be:

12 hours × £10 = £120 + 1/3 of 3 hours saved = 1 hour × £10

Total wage = £130

THINGS TO DO AND THINK ABOUT

1. Time-based Systems

From the following information, calculate the basic wages to be paid to each employee. The first one has been done for you.

Name	Basic Hours Worked	Hourly Rate per Hour	Weekly Wage
James Smith	35	£8	35 x £8 = £280
Alan Wilson	40	£10	
Lynn Thomson	38	£7.50	
Richard Bryson	35	£12	
Calum MacKay	38	£8.50	

2. Calculating Overtime Earnings

Copy and complete the following table to calculate the various overtime rates to be paid for each of the following basic rates of pay. The first one has been done for you.

Basic Rate	Time and 1/3	Time and 1/2	Double Time
£6	£8	£9	£12
£8			
£12			
£15			
£21			

DON'T FORGET

Labour remuneration is one of the three main costs to a business – it is important that accounting procedures are in place to accurately record and monitor labour costs.

ONLINE

Learn more about labour remuneration by completing the exercises at www.brightredbooks.net/N5Accounting

ONLINE TEST

Test your knowledge of labour remuneration at www.brightredbooks.net/N5Accounting

OVERHEADS

KEY TERMINOLOGY

Overheads

These are **indirect costs** which are **not** easily identifiable in the product being made – but without these costs, the product could not be made. Examples of overheads are:

- rent and rates
- heating and light
- cleaning
- electricity
- insurance
- factory maintenance.

Cost Unit

This is the item which the business is trying to work out the cost of producing. Examples are:

- loaf of bread
- tin of beans
- meal served in a restaurant
- tyre for a car
- television set
- operation in a hospital
- pint of beer.

Cost Allocation

Whole items of overhead costs can be allocated or 'charged' to a particular cost centre. For example, if the school canteen is treated as a cost centre, then the cleaning costs of the canteen would be charged directly to that cost centre.

Cost Apportionment

Where an overhead cannot be directly allocated or charged to one particular cost centre or department, the overhead will be apportioned (shared) between each cost centre or department that is responsible for the cost arising.

Cost Centre

This is a department or area of a business where costs can be gathered from or 'charged' to. Typical cost centres in a school could be:

- English Department
- Maths Department
- ICT Department
- School Office
- School Canteen
- Janitorial and Cleaning
- School Library.

The costs gathered from each cost centre can then be added to work out the total cost of running the school.

Typical cost centres in a factory producing cakes could be:

- Mixing
- Packaging
- Office and Administration
- Baking
- Storage.

Cost Absorption

Once all overheads have been charged to cost centres, a total overhead cost for the business or factory can be determined. The next stage is to charge each product (or cost unit) being made with a small proportion of the total overheads – this is known as overhead absorption.

EXAMPLE

If a factory makes 100 000 cakes in one year and the total overheads for the factory in that year are £50 000 then the overhead that would be absorbed onto each cake would be:

£50 000 / 100 000 cakes = 50p

Therefore, an overhead cost of 50p would be added on to the cost of producing each cake.

ALLOCATION AND APPORTIONMENT OF OVERHEADS

Methods of Overhead Apportionment

Floor Area	Number of Employees	Value of Fixed Assets	Power (metered)
Overheads are apportioned (shared) to cost centres based on the amount of floor space each cost centre or department takes up. This is suitable for overheads such as: • rent and rates • buildings insurance • lighting • cleaning of building • repairs and • maintenance of buildings.	Overheads are apportioned (shared) to cost centres based on the number of employees in each cost centre or department. This is suitable for overheads such as: • canteen costs • office and administration costs • personnel and staff welfare costs.	Overheads are apportioned (shared) to cost centres or departments based on the value of fixed assets in that cost centre. This method is used for the overhead of depreciation of fixed assets.	Overheads are apportioned (shared) to cost centres based on the amount of metered power the cost centre has used. This is suitable for overheads such as: • electricity • gas • water.

contd

EXAMPLE

Gowrie Cakes has two production departments: Baking and Finishing. The budgeted overheads are:

Rent   £15 000

Supervision   £18 000

The following information is also available:

	Baking	Finishing	Total
Floor area (sq m)	100	50	150
Number of employees	2	4	6

You are required to:

(a) select an appropriate basis of apportionment for each of the above overheads.

(b) use these to apportion each of the overheads between the departments.

(c) total the overheads apportioned to each department.

(d) total each overhead apportioned.

SOLUTION:

Gowrie Cakes

Overhead	Amount	Basis	Baking	Finishing
Rent	£15 000	Floor Area	£10 000	£5 000
Supervision	£18 000	No. of Employees	£6 000	£12 000
Total			£19 000	£14 000

Workings

Rent:	(£15 000/150) x 100
	(£15 000/150) x 50
Supervision:	(£18 000/6) x 2
	(£18 000/6) x 4

THINGS TO DO AND THINK ABOUT

1. Broomhead Plastics has two production departments (cost centres): Extrusion and Moulding.

    The budgeted overheads are:

    Lighting   £1200
    Vending machine costs   £900
    Insurance of equipment   £1800

    Additional information is available as follows:

	Extrusion	Moulding	Total
Floor area (sq m)	200	100	300
Number of employees	1	2	3
Value of equipment	£80 000	£40 000	£120 000

    You are required to:
    (a) select an appropriate basis of apportionment for each of the overheads.
    (b) use these to apportion (share) each of the overheads between the departments (cost centres).
    (c) total the overheads apportioned to each department.
    (d) total each overhead apportioned.

2. Fyvie Soap Works has two departments: Mixing and Moulding. The following information is available:

	Mixing	Moulding	Total
Floor area (sq m)	50	30	80
Value of equipment	£5 000	£3 000	£8 000
Value of buildings	£40 000	£60 000	£100 000
Number of employees	2	3	5

    The following are the budgeted overhead costs:

    Heating   £1600
    Depreciation of equipment   £2000
    Insurance of buildings   £200
    Staff supervision   £15 000

    You are required to:
    (a) select an appropriate basis of apportionment for each of the overheads.
    (b) use these to apportion each of the overheads between the departments.
    (c) total the overheads apportioned to each department.
    (d) total each overhead apportioned.

ONLINE

Learn more about overheads by completing the exercises at www.brightredbooks.net/N5Accounting

ONLINE TEST

Test your knowledge of overheads at www.brightredbooks.net/N5Accounting

ABSORPTION OF OVERHEADS

Once all overheads have been apportioned to cost centres or departments, the next stage is to find some suitable method for charging cost centre overheads onto the cost units – that is onto the final products being made.

There are **three main methods** for absorbing overheads onto cost units outlined below:

RATE PER UNIT PRODUCED

With this method, we take the total overheads for the cost centre (department) and divide them by the number of units the cost centre or department is expected to make.
This then gives an overhead charge for each unit produced.

$$\text{Formula} = \frac{\text{Total overheads}}{\text{Total units produced}}$$

EXAMPLE

$$\frac{£20\,000}{60\,000 \text{ units}}$$

$$= 33\text{p per unit}$$

MACHINE HOUR RATE

With this method, we take the total overheads for the cost centre (department) and divide them by the total number of machine hours the cost centre or department is expected to use throughout the year.
This then gives an overhead charge for each machine hour spent making the cost unit or product.

$$\text{Formula} = \frac{\text{Total overheads}}{\text{Total machine hours used}}$$

EXAMPLE

$$\frac{£80\,000}{20\,000 \text{ machine hours}}$$

$$= £4 \text{ per machine hour}$$

DIRECT LABOUR HOUR RATE

With this method, we take the total overheads for the cost centre (department) and divide them by the total number of labour hours the cost centre or department is expected to use throughout the year.
This then gives an overhead charge for each labour hour spent making the cost unit or product.

$$\text{Formula} = \frac{\text{Total overheads}}{\text{Total labour hours used}}$$

EXAMPLE

$$\frac{£120\,000}{60\,000 \text{ labour hours}}$$

$$= £2 \text{ per labour hour}$$

EXAMPLE

The following figures are available for the three production departments of Killin Toys.

Total	Dept A	Dept B	Dept C
Budgeted overhead	£40 000	£100 000	£30 000
Units produced	10 000	20 000	3000
Per unit			
Direct materials	£10	£12	£25
Direct wages	£20	£8	£18

You are required to calculate for each department:

(a) the absorption rate per unit.
(b) the total cost of making one unit.

SOLUTION:

Overhead absorption rate per unit:

DEPT A	DEPT B	DEPT C
$\dfrac{£40\,000}{10\,000 \text{ units}}$	$\dfrac{£100\,000}{20\,000 \text{ units}}$	$\dfrac{£30\,000}{3000 \text{ units}}$
£4 per unit	£5 per unit	£10 per unit

Total cost of making one unit:

DEPT A		**DEPT B**	
Direct materials	£10	Direct materials	£12
Direct wages	£20	Direct wages	£8
Overhead	£4	Overhead	£5
	£34		£25

DEPT C	
Direct Materials	£25
Direct Wages	£18
Overhead	£10
	£53

EXERCISE

The following figures for the three production departments of Comiston Products.

Total	Dept A	Dept B	Dept C
Budgeted overhead	£60 000	£90 000	£36 000
Units produced	30 000	30 000	15 000
Per unit			
Direct materials	£8	£11	£9
Direct wages	1 hour at £15 per hour	2 hours at £16 per hour	1.5 hours at £12 per hour

You are required to calculate for each department:

(a) the absorption rate per direct labour hour.
(b) the total cost of making one unit.

EXTENSION ✚

The material regarding the absorption of overheads is extension knowledge which will be useful if you go on to study Higher Accounting.

SERVICE COST CENTRES

So far, we have dealt with **production department cost centres**. However, all businesses are likely to have **service cost centres**, for example Maintenance or Administration Departments (cost centres). These departments exist for the whole business and to offer support or 'service' to the production cost centres. the overheads of service cost centres must therefore be **apportioned** among the production cost centres, again using a suitable basis.

EXAMPLE

APPORTIONMENT OF SERVICE COST CENTRES

C Kelly, a sole trader, has two production and two service departments. The factory overhead expenses incurred for the month of August were as follows:

	PRODUCTION DEPARTMENTS		SERVICE DEPARTMENTS	
	Mixing	Packaging	Maintenance	Personnel
Indirect labour	18 750	9 630	8 700	900
Indirect material	6 540	5 620	2 600	350
Heat, power	4 110	2 750	3 400	250
TOTAL	£29 400	£18 000	£14 700	£1 500
Bases for distribution:				
				TOTAL
No. of Employees	53	27	20	100
Maintenance man-hours	17	8		25

You are required to prepare a distribution of service department overheads to production departments.

SOLUTION:

		Production Cost Centres		Service Cost Centres	
		Mixing	Packaging	Maintenance	Personnel
		£29 400	£18 000	£14 700	£1 500
Personnel	£1 500	£795	£405	£300	
Main-tenance	£14 700	£9 996	£4 704		
TOTAL		£40 191	£23 109		

Personnel = (£1500/100 employees) x 53 employees

Personnel = (£1500/100 employees) x 27 employees

Personnel = (£1500/100 employees) x 20 employees

Maintenance = (£14 700/25 maintenance man hours) x 17 maintenance man hours for mixing

Maintenance = (£14 700/25 maintenance man hours) x 8 maintenance man hours for packaging

EXAMPLE

J Kerry is a sole trader, making and selling cakes. His factory consists of three production cost centres – mixing, firing and packaging. He also has two service cost centres – stores and cleaning.

The factory overhead expenses incurred for the month of August were as follows:

	Production Cost Centres			Service Cost Centres	
	Mixing	**Firing**	**Packaging**	**Stores**	**Administration**
Indirect labour	£3500	£4500	£6000	£1400	£800
Indirect materials	£12 000	£400	£4000	£100	£150
Rent	£50 000	£30 000	£30 000	£20 000	£5000
Heat and light	£4000	£10 000	£2000	£500	£1000
TOTALS	**£69 500**	**£44 900**	**£42 000**	**£22 000**	**£6 950**

You are required to prepare an overhead analysis schedule to show a distribution of service department overheads to production departments.

Basis of Apportionment:	
Number of employees:	**Floor Area:**
Mixing 10	Mixing 50 (Sq m)
Firing 5	Firing 25 (Sq m)
Packaging 5	Packaging 75 (Sq m)

Administration services the other four cost centres and so it should be re-apportioned first.

Stores only service the three production cost centres.

DON'T FORGET

The Personnel Department serves the other three departments and should be apportioned first on the basis of the number of employees. The Maintenance Department serves the production departments only.

ONLINE

Learn more about the absorption of overheads by completing the exercises at www.brightredbooks.net/N5Accounting

ONLINE TEST

Test your knowledge of absorption of overheads at www.brightredbooks.net/N5Accounting

THINGS TO DO AND THINK ABOUT

1. Define what is meant by an overhead.
2. List four examples of overheads.
3. Explain the difference between a cost centre and a cost unit.
4. Some overheads require to be apportioned.
   Explain the meaning of the term overhead apportionment.
5. Describe the difference between a production cost centre and a service cost centre.

JOB COSTING

WHAT IS JOB COSTING?

Job costing is a method of costing used where work consists of a number of individual jobs, which are normally completed to a customer's specific requirements. Examples might include:

- designing and fitting a kitchen to a customer's requirements
- landscaping a garden
- repairing a motor car.

The customer will ask the business to provide an estimate of cost for completing a piece of work or job. The main items of cost are:

- **Material** – materials can be costed very accurately to each job.
- **Labour** – as jobs are all unique and specific to individual customer's requirements, and approximate charge for labour can be given.
- **Overheads** – a charge for overheads will be added onto each job.
- **Selling and distribution overheads** – a share of these costs will also be charged to each job.

To keep a record of all costs in completing a specific job for a customer, a job cost card/sheet will be used.

EXAMPLE

An example of a job cost sheet is shown below:

Job Cost Card		Job No	234
Name of Customer: Mrs C Kelly			**Total Cost**
MATERIALS			
Quantity	Price per unit	Cost	
10	£50	£500	
6	£100	£600	£1100
LABOUR			
Hours	Rate per hour	Cost	
100	£10	£1000	
			£1000
OTHER DIRECT COSTS			
Hire of a special machine to complete job			
			£500
PRIME COSTS*			£2600
OVERHEADS	**Rate**	**Cost**	
Machining Dept – 60 hours	£1.80	£108	
Finishing Dept – 20 hours	£1.60	£32	
			£140
Selling and distribution costs			£50
Administration			£20
TOTAL COSTS			£2810
PROFIT (20%)			£562
CHARGE TO CUSTOMER			£3372

*PRIME COST = the total of direct material + direct labour + direct expenses.

PROFIT OR 'MARK-UP'

Once the cost of materials, labour and all overheads have been charged to the job and recorded on the job cost sheet, the total cost of the job will have been determined. The business will then add a percentage or 'mark-up' on to the total cost to incorporate their profit and determine the final selling price to be charged to the customer.

⚙ EXERCISE

Try out the following exercises:

1. A business's profit is calculated using a mark-up of 25% to the cost of each job. Calculate the profit and the selling price of each of the following jobs. The first one has been done for you.

Job No.	Cost	Profit
111	£200	£50
112	£460	
113	£500	
114	£600	

2. A business adds 50% to the cost of each job as their profit. Calculate the profit and the selling price of each of the following jobs:

Job No.	Cost
211	£2000
212	£4600
213	£5000
214	£6000

3. A business's profit is calculated using a profit margin of 25% on each job completed in their factory. Calculate the profit and cost for each of the following:

Job No.	Cost Price
500	£3000
501	£7500
502	£9000
503	£4500

contd

EXAMPLE

JOB COSTING

From the following information calculate the selling price of Job 10:

- Material £200
- Direct labour 20 hours at £6.00 per hour
- Hire of special tool £20
- Fixed overheads are recovered at £5 per direct labour hour
- Standard delivery charge: £20
- Add VAT at 20 %

The firm marks up the cost of each job by 40%.

SOLUTION:

	£		£
Direct material	200		
Direct labour	180		
Overheads (20 hours x £5)		100	
Hire of special tool	20		
PRIME COST			
Delivery charge			20
			500
			520
Mark-up (40%)			208
			728
VAT (20%)			145.60
Selling price			873.60

THINGS TO DO AND THINK ABOUT

Assignment – Overhead Analysis and Job Costing

PART A

From the following information you are required to prepare an overhead analysis statement for T Kelly and Son, showing clearly the apportionment of overheads, the bases used and all totals.

Budgeted overheads:

	£
Lighting and heating	1 100
Depreciation of plant	600
Rent and rates	1500
Insurance of plant	150
Plant repairs	750
Vending machines	1200

Additional information:

	Department A	Department B	Department C
Number of employees	5	4	1
Value of plant	£5000	£2500	-
Floor area	50%	40%	10%

Department C is a service department and its total overheads should be re-apportioned between the production departments on the basis of number of employees.

PART B

The absorption rate in Department A is based on direct labour hours and in Department B on machine hours. These rates are shown below:

Department A Absorption Rate	Department B Absorption Rate
£3.10 per direct labour hour	£3.60 per machine hour

PART C

Prepare a job cost statement for Job 25 using the information below, the absorption rates from **PART B** and adding a mark-up of 25% on cost for profit.

	Department A	Department B
Materials	20 m at £12 per m	3 m at £15 per m
Direct wages	16 hours at £20 per hour	3 hours at £18.50 per hour
Number of machine hours	5	2

CASH BUDGETS

WHAT IS A CASH BUDGET?

A budget is a **plan** of how much money a business has and how they will spend it.

The Management Accountant is responsible for ensuring that the business has sufficient cash funds flowing into the business to meet all cash payments. Preparing a cash budget should mean that:

- the business finances are better controlled and monitored and any unnecessary expenditure can be eliminated.
- the business can see where problems in its cash flow will arise, e.g. is there likely to be a shortage of cash in any particular month or months?
- decisions can be taken about purchasing large items which may require a lot of cash, e.g. the best time to make a big outlay of cash for non-current assets such as motor vehicles or machinery, etc.

As the cash budget is prepared ahead of time, sometimes, due to external and unexpected factors, the budget does not go completely to plan.

A cash budget:

- shows how much cash the organisation will have available, generally on a month to month basis;
- shows what money is expected to come in to the business during that time;
- shows what money is expected to get spent during that time;
- alerts the business to any cash flow problems;
- is used to help management make decisions;
- can be used to forecast whether a loan or overdraft may be necessary and if so when.

PREPARING A CASH BUDGET

A cash budget begins with the opening balance. This is the amount expected to be available to the firm at the start of the month. The next step is to anticipate the receipts for the month and add to the opening balance. Then payments forecasted to be made by the firm are taken away. This gives the closing balance. This is the amount of money left at the end of the month.

EXAMPLE

The following example explains and illustrates the layout of a cash budget. The information is for Sean Devine, a sole trader, and applies to the first four months of the year:

Cash Budget for Sean Devine – 20..				
	Jan	Feb	March	April
Opening Cash and Cash Equivalents Balance	6 000	−2 200	−5 400	−2 850
Money In				
Cash Sales	600	600	650	700
Credit Sales	4 000	4 000	5 400	5 400
	10 600	2 400	650	3 250
Money Out				
Purchases	2 000	2 000	2 500	3 000
Advertising	300	300	300	300
Wages	500	500	500	500
Rent	6 000			
Fixtures and Fittings	4 000			
Delivery Van		5 000		
Electricity			200	
	12 800	7 800	3 500	3 800
Closing Cash and Cash Equivalents Balance	−2 200	−5 400	−2 850	−550

The **opening balance** is the amount of money in the bank or in cash in the business at the start of the month. This is added to the **total cash in.** This is any money received into the business, e.g. from selling goods – or any other sources. This gives the total cash available for that month. Then, cash out (any amounts paid out of the business) is taken away. This gives the **closing balance** – the amount of money left in the business at the end of the months trading. **The closing balance at the end of one month is the opening balance for the next month.**

USING THE CASH BUDGET

Using the example above, Sean can now use the cash budget to plan ahead and to help make decisions. More importantly, he will not run the risk of being unable to pay his bills. For example, suppose Sean has decided that in February he wants to buy a new delivery van for the business.

The total cost of the delivery van will be £5000. By planning ahead and looking at his cash flow, he realises that he cannot afford it just now as he does not have enough cash to buy it. Therefore, to ensure his business does not get into cash flow problems, he could consider:

- getting a **loan** for the van – by applying for a loan Sean could get the van straight away and pay it off month by month. However, interest would have to be paid to the bank in addition to the repayments for the loan.
- buying the van on **credit** – again Sean could get the van straight away but usually he would have to pay interest along with the monthly repayments.

- Lease – Sean could lease the van. A lease is a kind of agreement to 'rent' a van from a hire company. Sean would make monthly payments for the use of the van. While the van will never belong to him, he is not responsible for the maintenance of the van or any repairs which may be necessary.

The cash budget is therefore used for decision-making in businesses. It shows whether there is enough money for the business to do what it plans. It can also show whether a business needs to find cash from somewhere else. It can help a business answer questions like:

- Do I need to arrange an overdraft/loan?
- Do I have enough money to buy a new piece of equipment?
- Is there enough cash flowing into the business to allow the business to pay its overheads and other costs?

 THINGS TO DO AND THINK ABOUT

It is vital that cash comes into a business to ensure good cash flow. Therefore, accountants need to calculate both cash and credit sales.

1. From the following information, calculate cash and credit sales units and the sales revenues for inclusion in the cash budget for the three-month period February–April for N Bates:
   - unit selling price £100
   - credit customers receive trade discount of 40% and pay two months after delivery
   - cash customers receive an additional discount of 5%

Estimated sales amount to:

December	January	February	March	April
13000	11000	9000	8000	10000

N Bates estimates that 80% of all sales will be on credit.

2. From the following information, calculate cash and credit sales units and the sales revenues for inclusion in the cash budget for the three-month period February–April for O King.
   - unit selling price £200
   - credit customers receive trade discount of 50% and pay two months after delivery.
   - cash customers receive an additional discount of 5%

Estimated sales amount to:

December	January	February	March	April
20000	18000	12000	14000	16000

O King estimates that 60% of all sales will be on credit.

 DON'T FORGET

An overdraft allows you to spend or take out more cash than you have in a current account.

 **VIDEO**

Learn more about cash budgeting by watching the clip at www.brightredbooks.net/N5Accounting

 ONLINE TEST

Test your knowledge of cash budgeting at www.brightredbooks.net/N5Accounting

CASH FLOW PROBLEMS

INTRODUCTION

Cash flow problems can arise even if the firm is successful in selling a lot of its goods. If goods are being sold on credit, customers do not pay for their goods straight away. This can lead to cash flow problems as the company is having to pay for their stock and overheads (for example heat, light, petrol, rent and wages) before their customers are paying for the goods sold to them.

Therefore, it is vital that cash flow is well controlled to make sure the business is successful. As a result, the business should consider the following and make the necessary decisions to minimise the risk:

- Timing of flows of cash into and out of a firm is crucial. It is as important as the total amount of cash generated.
- Sole traders who make sure that they always have enough cash available for their needs are more likely to be successful and ensure survival.

METHODS OF IMPROVING CASH FLOW

There are a lot of decisions a firm can make to improve their cash flow. Doing this can help them to avoid cash flow problems. The kinds of things, which help to improve cash flow, include:

- **Raising extra capital** – re-investing profits or the owner investing more funds. By doing this, the firm will get an inflow of cash.
- **Taking out loans** – from a bank or small organisations or from friends or family. By doing this, the organisation will get an inflow of cash but repayments (including interest) will have to be made regularly.
- **Tight credit control** – this means that the sole trader should ensure that he/she collects the money owing from trade receivables (people who owe the business money) as quickly as possible. This will improve the inflow of money but may cause bad feelings with customers who may leave and go to other suppliers.
- **Delaying payment** – taking longer to pay bills or invoices for purchases of stock. By doing this, the organisation will reduce the outflow of cash until cash has been received from customers. However, this may upset some creditors who wish to get their money as quickly as possible.
- **Spreading purchase costs** – hire purchase or leasing. This will mean that the outflow of cash will not all be in one month but will be spread over a number of months or years.
- **Tight stock control** – ensure capital is not tied up in too much stock. This will ensure that the outflow of cash is kept to a reasonable level.

CASH FLOW PROBLEM	POSSIBLE SOLUTION
Not enough to pay wages	Overdraft facility offered by the bank
Need new equipment	Leasing
Cannot afford to buy more stock	Buy on credit – pay later
No money for bills	Offer (trade receivables) debtors incentives to pay quickly
Want to buy new premises	Loan
Expenses are too high	A range of cost cutting procedures, e.g. ensure you are on the best rates for electricity, only use phone at certain times, etc.

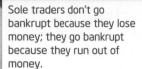

DEALING WITH RECEIPTS FROM CASH AND CREDIT SALES

EXAMPLE

From the following information, calculate cash and credit sales units and sales revenues for inclusion in the cash budget for the three-month period February–April for Jackson Hill.

- unit selling price £50
- credit customers receive trade discount of 30% and pay one month after delivery
- cash customers receive an additional discount of 5%

Estimated sales amount to:

January	February	March	April
10 000	12 000	14 000	10 000

Jackson Hill estimates that 75% of all sales will be on credit.

SOLUTION:

Jackson Hill

Extract from cash budget for February–April

Receipts	February	March	April
Credit Sales	£262 500	£315 000	£367 500
Cash Sales	£97 500	£113 750	£81 250
Total Receipts	£360 000	£428 750	£448 750

Calculation of Cash Sales

February (12 000 × 25%) × £50 × 35 %
March (14 000 × 25%) × £50 × 35 %
April (10 000 × 25%) × £50 × 35 %

Calculation of Credit Sales

February (£10 000 × 75%) × 30 %
March (£12 000 × 75%) × 30 %
April (£14 000 × 75%) × 30 %

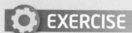 EXERCISE

From the following information, calculate cash and credit sales units and sales revenues for inclusion in the cash budget for the three-month period July–September for John McGhee:

- unit selling price £400
- credit customers receive trade discount of 25% and pay one month after delivery
- cash customers receive an additional discount of 10%

Estimated sales amount to:

June	July	August	September
120 000	130 000	100 000	150 000

John McGhee estimates that 65% of all sales will be on credit.

 ONLINE TEST

Test your knowledge of cash flow problems at www.brightredbooks.net/N5Accounting

 THINGS TO DO AND THINK ABOUT

R Jeeves has exactly £1 000 cash with which to start a business. He has also received permission from a bank manager to have an overdraft of up to £10 000 during his first six months of business starting 1 January.

His plans for the first six months trading are:

1. Payments for goods and supplies – Jan £5500, Feb £7 200, March £9 700, April £10 500, May £9 600, June £6 900.
2. Receipts from debtors will be – Jan £3 900, Feb £5 900, March £6000, April £7 100, May £8 400, June £9500.
3. Loan receivable on 1 March £700 to be repaid in full plus £100 interest on 1 June.
4. Drawings per calendar month £300.

You are required to draw up a cash budget for the six months showing the balances each month and to make any suitable comments.

CASH BUDGETS AND SPREADSHEETS

ONLINE

Learn about sales and production budgets at www.brightredbooks.net

WHY USE SPREADSHEETS?

Spreadsheets can be used to prepare cash budgets more efficiently. Once formulae have been entered into the spreadsheet, the business can 'experiment' with different figures for selling price per unit, material cost per unit and business expenses to identify the impact on cash flow.

EXAMPLE

Look at this simple example:

	A	B	C	D
1	John Craig			
2	Cash Budget for three months January–March			
3				
4		January	February	March
5	OPENING CASH AND CASH EQUIVALENTS	£25000	=B21	=C21
6				
7	RECEIPTS			
8	Cash Sales	£50000	£40000	£60000
9	Credit Sales	£120000	£110000	£90000
10	Loan		£50000	
11	TOTAL RECEIPTS	=SUM(B8:B10)	=SUM(C8:C10)	=SUM(D8:D10)
12				
13	PAYMENTS			
14	Materials	£8000	£12000	£16000
15	Labour	£20000	£18000	£24000
16	Variable Overhead	£6000	£8000	£12000
17	Fixed Costs	£10000	£10000	£10000
18	Loan Interest		£1500	
19	TOTAL PAYMENTS	=SUM(B14:B18)	=SUM(C14:C18)	=SUM(D14:D18)
20				
21	CLOSING CASH AND CASH EQUIVALENTS	=(B5+B11)-B19	=(C5+C11)-C19	=(D5+D11)-D19
22				

EXERCISE 1

Draw up a cash budget for N Norris showing the balance at the end of each month, from the following information for the six months ended 31 December Year 11.

1. Opening cash and cash equivalents £1200.

Production in units:

Year 11									Year 12	
APR	MAY	JUN	JUL	AUG	SEP	OCT	NOV	DEC	JAN	FEB
240	270	300	320	350	370	380	340	310	260	250

2. Raw materials used in production cost £5 per unit. Of this 80% is paid in the month of production and 20% in the month after production.
3. Direct labour costs of £8 per unit are payable in the month of production.
4. Variable expenses are £2 per unit, payable one half in the same month as production and one half in the month following production.

Sales at £20 per unit:

Year 11									
MAR	APR	MAY	JUN	JUL	AUG	SEP	OCT	NOV	DEC
260	200	320	290	400	300	350	400	390	400

5. Trade receivables will pay their accounts three months after that in which sales are made.
6. Fixed expenses of £400 per month are payable each month.
7. Machinery costing £2000 to be paid for in October Year 11.
8. Norris will receive a legacy in December Year 11 of £2500.
9. Drawings will be £300 per month.

contd

EXERCISE 2

Draw up a cash budget for J Clarke from the following information for the six months 1 July–31 December Year 11.
1. Opening cash and cash equivalents £1500.
Sales at £20 per unit:

APR	MAY	JUN	JUL	AUG	SEP	OCT	NOV	DEC
110	120	140	160	180	190	130	80	70

2. Trade receivables will pay two months after they have bought the goods.
Production in units:

APR	MAY	JUN	JUL	AUG	SEP	OCT	NOV	DEC	JAN
150	170	180	200	130	110	100	90	70	60

3. Raw materials cost £6 per unit and are paid for three months after the goods are used in production.
4. Direct labour of £5 per unit is payable in the same month as production.
5. Other variable expenses are £3 per unit. Two thirds of this cost is paid for in the same month as production and one third in the month following production.
6. Fixed expenses of £150 per month are paid one month in arrears – these expenses have been at this rate for the past 2 years.
7. A machine is to be bought and paid for in September for £6000.
8. Clarke will borrow £3000 from a relative in December. This will be put into the business bank account immediately.

EXERCISE 3

D Smith is to open a retail shop on 1 January. He will put in £25 000 cash as equity. His plans are as follows:
1. On 1 January he will buy and pay for premises of £20 000, shop fixtures of £3000 and a motor van £1000.
2. He will employ two assistants, each to get a salary of £130 per month, to be paid at the end of each month.
He will buy the following goods (in units):

JAN	FEB	MAR	APR	MAY	JUN
200	220	280	350	400	330

He will sell the following number of units:

JAN	FEB	MAR	APR	MAY	JUN
120	180	240	300	390	420

3. Units will be sold for £10 each. One-third of sales are for cash, the other two-thirds being on credit. These latter customers are expected to pay their accounts in the second month following that in which they received the goods.
The units will cost £6 each for January–April inclusive, and £7 each thereafter. Trade payables will be paid in the month following purchase.
4. The other expenses of the shop will be £150 per month payable in the month following that in which they were incurred.
5. Part of the premises will be sub-let as an office at a rent of £600 per annum. This is paid in equal instalments in March, June, September and December.
6. Smith's cash drawings will amount to £250 per month.
7. You are required to show a cash budget for the six months to the end of June.

THINGS TO DO AND THINK ABOUT

EXTENSION TASK

Frank Buchanan is starting a removal firm business called Move-it. The following details relate to the first four months of business for June–September Year 1.

(a) Move-it start with £150 000 in their business bank account.
(b) They have agreed to purchase two removal vans costing £50 000 each, paid for in July.
(c) They agree to purchase premises costing £300 000. After an initial deposit of £100 000 paid in June, they remainder will be paid in 20 equal instalments starting in July.
(d) Rates for their premises will be £6000 per annum, paid monthly.
(e) They estimate that they will make the following number of removals during the next four months.

	June	July	Aug	Sept
Removals	20	22	25	30

(f) The average charge per customer removal is £1500. Customers pay a deposit of £500 in the month of the removal and the remainder in the month following the removal.
(g) They estimate the average mileage for each removal is 400 miles.
(h) Fuel costs are 5p per mile and are paid for in the month incurred.

(i) Licences will be £1200 per vehicle paid in June.
(j) Insurance per vehicle will be £2000 per annum. This is paid quarterly and the first payment is to be made in June.
(k) Two drivers are employed and are paid £50 each per removal, paid in the month the work is carried out.
(l) Expenses for each driver averages £20 per removal. The expenses are paid to the drivers in the month following the removal.
(m) Service costs amount to £400 per quarter per removal van, with the first service due in August.
(n) Administration costs amount to £100 per month.
(o) Packaging materials will be £50 per removal. Suppliers of the packaging material are paid in the month following the removal.
(p) Fixed overheads amount to £1000 per month. This figure includes depreciation of £400.
(q) In August they will complete a removal abroad at a special price of £4300. Special costs incurred will be £1500 and will be paid in the month of removal. The customer will pay a deposit of £1000 in July and the remainder in September.

Prepare the cash budget for the four months June–September.

DON'T FORGET

Depreciation costs do not involve any actual movement of cash and so it does not appear in a cash budget. Depreciation involves writing down the value of an asset but there is no actual payment of cash for depreciation.

VIDEO

Find out more about cash flow by watching the video at www.brightredbooks.net/N5Accounting

ONLINE TEST

Test your knowledge of cash flow and spreadsheets at www.brightredbooks.net/N5Accounting

EXTENSION TASKS ON CASH BUDGETING

Now that you have learned all about cash budgeting, test yourself with these extension tasks!

 EXERCISE

EXTENSION TASK 1

The following estimates have been prepared for John Brown, a sole trader:

1. Cash and cash equivalents balance on 1 October to be £35 000.

2. Production for the 6-month period August–January is:

Aug	Sept	Oct	Nov	Dec	Jan
4000	4100	3600	3900	4100	4500

3. Sales revenue for the 6-month period August–January is:

Aug	Sept	Oct	Nov	Dec	Jan
4000	4100	3500	3800	4200	4400

4. Unit selling price is to be £150 less 20% trade discount for credit customers. Cash customers receive an additional discount of 5%, that is they receive a 25% trade discount.

5. Credit sales account for 80% of all sales.

6. Customers settle their accounts one month after sale.

7. Raw materials cost £40 per unit less 10% trade discount. These are paid for in the month after production.

8. Direct labour is £10 per unit and is paid in the same month as the units are produced.

9. Variable production costs amount to £5 per unit and are paid in the month incurred.

10. Monthly fixed costs, including depreciation of £1500, are to be £13 500.

11. The firm intends to purchase machinery costing £250 000 in October. This is to be paid for in five monthly instalments beginning in November.

You are required to:

1. Calculate the cash and credit selling price (ignore VAT).

2. Prepare a monthly cash budget for the three months October–December.

3. From your cash budget state whether John Brown will have a cash flow problem during the three months.

4. If so suggest one reason for this and how this could be overcome.

 EXERCISE

EXTENSION TASK 2

1. The following estimates have been prepared for S Black, a sole trader: Cash and cash equivalents balance on 1 June to be £50 000

2. Sales revenue for the 6-month period April–September:

April	May	June	July	Aug	Sept
6000	7000	6400	7000	7600	6600

Production for the 6-month period April–September:

April	May	June	July	Aug	Sept
6000	7000	6600	7000	7600	6600

3. Unit selling price to regular trade customers is to be £55.

4. All sales are on credit and cash discount for payment within one month is 5%.

5. On average 50% of customers make payment one month after sales. The remaining customers pay two months after sales.

6. Raw materials are paid for two months after production. The cost is £35 per unit.

7. Direct labour is £12 per unit and is paid in the same month as the units are produced.

DON'T FORGET

Closing balance for one month must equal the opening balance of the next month.

contd

8. A production bonus of £2 per unit is paid for in any month where production exceeds 6800 units. The bonus is paid the following month.

9. Variable production costs amount to £4 per unit and are paid in the month incurred.

10. Monthly fixed costs are estimated to be £30 000.

11. S Black intends to replace its fleet of salesmen's cars in June at a cost of £100 000. A deposit of £40 000 will be paid in June and the remainder in 10 equal instalments starting in July.

You are required to:

1. Calculate the unit selling price for one-month customers and two-month customers (ignore VAT)

2. Prepare a monthly cash budget for the three months June–August

3. From your cash budget state whether S Black will experience a cash flow problem during the 3-month period.

4. If so suggest one reason for this and how it could be overcome.

EXERCISE

EXTENSION TASK 3

The following estimates have been prepared for O King who is a sole trader:

1. Cash and cash equivalents balance on 1 Jan to be £30 000.

2. Sales revenue is estimated to be:

Jan	Feb	Mar	Apr	May	June
5000	5000	5500	5500	6000	6000

Production is estimated to be:

Jan	Feb	Mar	Apr	May	June
5000	5000	5100	5600	6000	6000

3. Unit selling price to regular credit customers is to be £40 less 10% trade discount. Credit customers settle their accounts in the month following sales.

4. Cash customers collect their own goods and it is estimated that 50% of sales will be for cash and these customers receive 15% cash discount.

5. Variable unit costs are: material £6, labour £25, production overheads £12, selling and distribution overheads are £3 per unit.

6. Fixed costs, including depreciation of £1000, are £4000.

7. Material suppliers are paid two months after the materials are used in production.

8. Wages are paid in the month the units are made.

9. Variable production overheads are paid in the month following production.

10. Variable selling and distribution overheads are paid two months after delivery.

11. O King plans to replace some of her plant and machinery. She intends to sell two machines in March and expects to receive £60 000 in total. These will be replaced by two new machines costing £90 000 each. An initial deposit of £48 000 will be paid in April, the remainder being paid off (in equal instalments) over four months starting in May.

12. To help pay for these machines, O King has arranged a bank loan of £50 000 receivable in April. Interest at the rate of 5% per annum starting in May.

You are required to:

1. Calculate the unit selling price for cash and credit customers (ignore VAT).

2. Prepare a monthly cash budget for the three months March–May.

3. Comment on O King's cash flow.

THINGS TO DO AND THINK ABOUT

PROGRESS CHECK

1. Explain the main difference between the role of the financial accountant and the management accountant.
2. List the main duties that are likely to be undertaken by a financial accountant.
3. Outline some tasks that may be undertaken by a management accountant.
4. State two examples of the type of work that job costing is usually applied to.
5. Explain what is meant by the term 'mark-up'.
6. Define the meaning of prime cost.
7. Explain why a sole trader would be well advised to prepare a cash budget.
8. Outline four strategies that could be used to improve the cash flow of a sole trader.

ONLINE TEST

Test your knowledge of cash budgeting at www. brightredbooks.net/ N5Accounting

INVESTIGATING ACCOUNTS

THE ACCOUNTANT AS AN INVESTIGATOR!

All sole traders will normally prepare an income statement and a statement of financial position at the end of each financial year. In Unit 1, we looked at the preparation of both of these accounting statements. Careful study and analysis of these final accounting statements can provide an enormous amount of information about the performance of a business organisation. By interpreting all the accounting information available and making comparisons with figures for previous years, figures for similar organisations or by analysing the relationship between different figures, it is possible to find the real indicators of the future success and financial stability of an organisation.

The types of questions that can be answered by interpretation of the final accounts income statement and statement of financial position are explained further below.

Income Statement

- Is this year's sales figure higher than the previous year's sales figure or higher than the sales figures of rival businesses?
- Has the gross profit improved this year, compared with last year?
- Is the business earning a higher gross profit than rival businesses?
- Is the business turning over sufficient amounts of stock? In simple terms, is the business's stock proving popular with customers?
- Has the profit for the year improved this year, compared with last year?
- Does the business's profit for the year figure compare favourably with those of other organisations in the same line of business?

Statement of Financial Position

- Do we have enough working capital (current assets – current liabilities) to avoid cash flow problems?
- Is the equity invested in the business relatively secure and generating a satisfactory return?
- Is the business making enough use of available trade credit?
- Are non-current assets working to generate income for the business?
- Is our level of trade receivables comparable with that of our competitors?
- Are trade receivables being encouraged to pay promptly?

 **EXERCISE 1**

Revision Questions

1. Outline the purpose of preparing an income statement.
2. State when a business would prepare such an account.
3. In your own words, explain what you understand by the following accounting terms found in an income statement:
   - sales revenue or turnover
   - cost of sales
   - gross profit
   - profit for the year

4. List three examples of expenses that you might find in an income statement.
5. Explain the difference between gross profit and profit for the year.

contd

EXERCISE 2

Revision Task

The following trial balance was extracted from the ledger accounts of V Taylor on 31 December Year 2 along with the accompanying notes.

Trial Balance as at 31 December Year 2		
	Dr	Cr
	£	£
Sales Revenue		640 000
Purchases	290 000	
Opening Inventory	15 920	
Carriage inwards	1 450	
Carriage outwards	1 800	
Discount received		1 320
Discount allowed	2 300	
Commission received		2 600
Rent and rates	2 100	
Wages	120 000	
Insurance	1 500	
Trade Receivables and Trade Payables	8 200	5 600
Cash and Cash Equivalents	12 500	
VAT		2 750
Premises	200 000	
Office equipment	15 000	
Machinery	120 000	
Provision for Depreciation:		
Office equipment		3 500
Machinery		43 200
Drawings	22 500	
Equity		114 300
	813 270	813 270

Notes at 31 October Year 2:

1. Closing Inventory: £13 500.
2. Accruals: Wages £3200, Rent and rates £300.
3. Prepaid insurance £200.
4. Commission received of £200 has still to be received.
5. Write off another 5% deprecation from office equipment and machinery.

You are required to prepare the income statement for the year and statement of financial position as at 31 December Year 2.

THINGS TO DO AND THINK ABOUT

Once you have prepared the income statement for a sole trader, you will then prepare a statement of financial position for the year end. There are items which appear in the income statement that will also appear in the statement of financial position, for example, closing inventory. You should list other items that will be taken from the income statement to the statement of financial position.

DON'T FORGET

The purpose of the income statement is to calculate gross profit and profit for the year.

CALCULATING ACCOUNTING RATIOS

INTRODUCTION

In order to guard the long-term security of a small business (sole trader), the owner must pay close attention to the following three areas:

- Profitability – Is the organisation earning more income than it is paying out?
- Liquidity – Does the organisation have enough money to pay its debts and regular bills?
- Efficiency – Is the organisation making the best use of its non-current assets and other resources?

REASONS FOR USING ACCOUNTING RATIOS

- To compare the current year's income statement and statement of financial position to those of previous years.
- To compare the business's income statement and statement of financial position to those of other firms in the same line of business.
- To provide information for interested parties. For example, lenders like banks would be interested in a business's liquidity and profitability before offering a loan.
- To provide information which may be of interest to trade payables or potential investors.
- To identify any problem areas within the business in order that they can be addressed.

RATIOS THAT MEASURE PROFITABILITY

$$Gross\ Profit\ Percentage\ (GP\%) = \frac{Gross\ Profit}{Sales\ Revenue} \times 100\% = \%$$

$$Profit\ for\ the\ Year\ \% = \frac{Profit\ for\ the\ Year}{Sales\ Revenue} \times 100\% = \%$$

$$Return\ on\ Equity\ Employed = \frac{Profit\ for\ the\ Year}{Opening\ Equity} \times 100 =$$

RATIOS THAT MEASURE LIQUIDITY

Current Ratio (Working Capital Ratio)

$$Current\ Assets : Current\ Liabilities = \frac{CA}{CL} = ratio\ e.g.2{:}1$$

RATIOS THAT MEASURE EFFICIENCY

$$Rate\ of\ Inventory\ Turnover = \frac{Cost\ of\ Sales}{Average\ Stock} = Times\ sold$$

$$*Av\ (Inventory)\ Stock = \frac{Opening\ Inventory + Closing\ Inventory}{2}$$

$$Expenses\ Ratio = \frac{Expenses^*}{Sales\ Revenue} \times 100\% = \%$$

$$\begin{array}{c}Trade\ Receivables\\Collection\ Period\end{array} = \frac{Average\ Trade\ Receivables}{Total\ Credit\ Sales} \times 365 = days^*$$

$$\begin{array}{c}Trade\ Payables\\Payment\ Period\end{array} = \frac{Average\ Trade\ Payables}{Total\ Credit\ Purchases} \times 365 = days^*$$

$$\begin{array}{c}Non\text{-}current\ Assets\\Turnover\end{array} = \frac{Net\ Sales}{Non\text{-}current\ Assets\ at\ net\ book\ value} = ratio,\ e.g.\ 3{:}1$$

NOTE: RoIT can be expressed in days, weeks or months simply by multiplying the number of times the average stock is sold by 365 for answers in days, 52 for answers in weeks and 12 for answers in months.

* This figure may be for the total expenses or for one individual expense, e.g. advertising or wages.

* (or × 52 = weeks, or × 12 = months)
NOTE: where only one figure is given for trade receivables or trade payables, this will be taken as the average.

NOTE: Net sales is the sales figure after returns have been subtracted (turnover)

HOW TO IMPROVE BUSINESS RATIOS

Gross Profit % (GP%)

This can be improved by increasing a business's gross profit. A sole trader may find the following strategies to be effective:

- reduce cost of purchases by finding a cheaper supplier;
- reduce cost of purchases by buying in bulk and requesting discounts;
- cut down theft of inventory by staff/outsiders;
- increase the selling price of their products.

Profit for the Year %

This can be improved by increasing a business's profit for the year. A sole trader may find the following strategies to be effective:

- increase the gross profit using the methods outlined above;
- reduce expenses – transport, postage, heat and light, wages, etc.;
- pay suppliers promptly to receive cash discounts.

Return on Equity Employed

This ratio indicates the amount of profit that the sole trader has earned in return for investing equity in the business.

- Used for comparing the profitability of similar firms in the same line of business.
- This ratio improves when a business earns more profit for the year.

Current (Working Equity) Ratio

This ratio measures the firm's ability to pay its short-term debts when they are due. Generally, current assets should be twice as much as current liabilities (2:1). Potential creditors and lenders **will not support a firm** whose current liabilities are greater than its current assets.

- This ratio indicates whether the business has enough current assets to pay for current liabilities.
- Indicates whether or not the business has a liquidity or cash flow problem.
- Ideally trade receivables should be asked to pay before or at the same time as the business has to pay its trade payables.
- To improve this ratio, current assets should be increased and current liabilities should be decreased.

Expense Ratio

This ratio measures if expenses are too high in relation to sales. If expenses are too high the firm must find ways to reduce them in order to increase profit. This could mean taking action like making some staff redundant. Alternatively they could, if possible, increase sales revenue without increasing expenses.

Rate of Inventory Turnover (RoIT)

This ratio determines the number of times inventory is turned over within a financial year. Rate of inventory turnover may be improved by:

- Increasing sales by more advertising and better marketing techniques.
- Make use of special offers on slow selling products.
- Offer customers discounts for bulk purchases, to encourage customers to purchase more.
- Change to a supplier whose inventory may be more popular with customers.

Trade Receivables Collection Period

This ratio measures how long it takes the firm's trade receivables to pay. A healthy ratio would be approximately one month. To encourage trade receivables to pay more quickly, they could be offered a cash discount. Ideally trade receivables should pay before the business has to pay its trade payables. This can be improved by:

- increasing credit control/monitoring of outstanding invoices;
- sending out invoices promptly.

Trade Payables Payment Period

This ratio measures the length of time it takes a firm to pay trade payables. A long period could indicate that the business is experiencing poor cash flow or low sales. A healthy ratio would be approximately one month.

Non-current Asset Turnover Ratio

This ratio measures how well the business is using its non-current assets to generate sales revenue. If the ratio is high it shows the business is making good use of its non-current assets. If the ratio is low or decreasing, it may mean that non-current assets are becoming inefficient and need to be replaced or updated. It may also indicate that the business has too many non-current assets which are not really needed and so should be sold.

 THINGS TO DO AND THINK ABOUT

1. List those ratios that would be used to analyse an income statement.
2. List those ratios that would be used to analyse a statement of financial position.

 ONLINE TEST

Test your knowledge of accounting ratios at www.brightredbooks.net/N5Accounting

USING ACCOUNTING RATIOS

REASONS FOR LIQUIDITY PROBLEMS

- Too much cash tied up in inventory. When a sole trader 'over stocks', cash is not available for other financial commitments. Also, he/she runs the risk of not being able to sell the inventory if tastes and fashions change.
- Customers who are sold goods on credit (trade receivables) may have been given too long to pay.
- If trade receivables take too long to pay, day-to-day expenses may be greater than income generated from credit sales (e.g. trade payables may not be paid on time thereby losing out on cash discounts available).
- Prepayment of expenses such as insurance, rent, etc. means cash is being spent unnecessarily.
- Paying trade payables too soon – negotiate longer payment periods. This provides more time to sell inventory and generate cash and profit in which to pay trade payables.
- Current liabilities may be greater than current assets. Remember a business should always have twice as many current assets as it has liabilities, if it wishes to avoid liquidity problems.
- Non-current assets may have been purchased or large unexpected repairs paid thereby affecting liquidity by reducing the bank balance.
- The business may have purchased an expensive non-current asset which could have been hired or leased to prevent having to pay out large amounts of cash or taking on loans with heavy interest payments.

METHODS OF IMPROVING LIQUIDITY PROBLEMS

- Try to reduce bank overdrafts as they often incur high interest charges.
- The owner should invest more equity in the business to improve the availability of cash.
- Offer incentives to trade receivables to pay sooner to ensure the business is receiving payment promptly, for example, cash discounts.
- Sell off unused equipment and other non-current assets for cash.
- Reduce cash outlays temporarily by buying materials on credit instead of paying cash.
- Try to get a longer period of credit from suppliers, e.g. two months instead of one month.
- Reduce all business expenses where possible and avoid prepayments.
- Advertise to increase sales revenue and rate of inventory turnover to generate more sales revenue.

PARTIES WHO WOULD BE INTERESTED IN THE FIRM'S RATIOS ARE:

- The owner (sole trader) who wants to see how profitable their investment/business is.
- Potential trade payables (such as suppliers or banks) who would require to know if the business is able to repay any loans given.
- Employees who are interested in wage rates, bonuses, profit-sharing and job security would be interested in the profitability of the business.
- Investors or lenders who are interested in lending the business money would want to check on the profitability and efficiency of the business.

⚙ EXERCISE 1

Now try these exercises on accounting ratios.

V Galloway, a sole trader, wishes to assess her business's performance over the last 2 years using the following information.

Calculate the following ratios for each of the 2 years:

(a) Gross profit percentage
(b) Profit for the year percentage
(c) Return on equity employed
(d) Current ratio
(e) Rate of inventory turnover
(f) Expenses ratio

	Year 1	Year 2
	£000	£000
Sales Revenue (net)	450	640
Cost of Sales	300	390
Opening Inventory	38	42
Closing Inventory	46	52
Expenses	78	105
Opening Equity	360	440
Current Assets	220	250
Current Liabilities	80	50

contd

EXERCISE 2

D Jarvis, a sole trader, wishes to assess her business's performance over the last 2 years using the following information.

Calculate the following ratios for each of the 2 years:

(a) Gross profit percentage
(b) Profit for the year percentage
(c) Return on equity employed
(d) Current ratio
(e) Rate of inventory turnover
(f) Expenses ratio

	Year 1	Year 2
	£000	£000
Sales Revenue (net)	750	950
Cost of Sales	550	680
Opening Inventory	70	80
Closing Inventory	80	110
Expenses	140	180
Opening Equity	630	700
Current Assets	380	400
Current Liabilities	150	90

EXERCISE 3

S Devine, a sole trader, wishes to assess his business's performance over the last 2 years using the following information.

Calculate the following ratios for each of the 2 years:

(a) Gross profit percentage
(b) Profit for the year percentage
(c) Return on equity employed
(d) Current ratio
(e) Rate of inventory turnover
(f) Expenses ratio

	Year 1	Year 2
	£000	£000
Sales Revenue (net)	640	780
Cost of Sales	474	569
Opening Inventory	100	120
Closing Inventory	120	130
Expenses	104	139
Opening Equity	535	588
Current Assets	340	360
Current Liabilities	168	122

EXERCISE 4

L Taylor, a sole trader, wishes to assess her business's performance over the last 2 years using the following information.

Calculate the following ratios for each of the 2 years.

(a) Gross profit percentage
(b) Profit for the year percentage
(c) Return on equity employed
(d) Current ratio
(e) Rate of inventory turnover
(f) Expenses ratio

	Year 1	Year 2
	£000	£000
Sales Revenue (net)	620	748
Cost of Sales	400	500
Opening Inventory	46	55
Closing Inventory	55	62
Expenses	94	126
Opening Equity	432	558
Current Assets	200	210
Current Liabilities	96	60

THINGS TO DO AND THINK ABOUT

PROGRESS CHECK

1. Outline three reasons why a sole trader might encounter liquidity problems.
2. Suggest three actions that a sole trader could take to avoid liquidity problems.
3. List three parties who would be interested in the financial performance of a business and outline what their specific interest would be.

ONLINE TEST

Test your knowledge of accounting ratios at www.brightredbooks.net/N5Accounting

ONLINE

Practise further with extra accounting ratio exercises at www.brightredbooks.net/N5Accounting

FURTHER EXERCISES ON ACCOUNTING RATIOS

EXERCISE 1

Mark Cooper, a sole trader, wishes to assess his business's performance over the last 2 years using the following information.

	Year 1	Year 2
	£000s	£000s
Sales Revenue (net)	480	540
Cost of Sales	320	380
Opening inventory	48	60
Closing inventory	40	70
Gross profit	168	162
Profit for the year	72	54
Opening equity	450	522
Current assets	250	280
Current liabilities	80	100

Calculate the following ratios for both years:

(a) Gross profit %
(b) Profit for the year %
(c) Return on equity employed
(d) Current ratio
(e) Rate of inventory turnover
(f) Expenses ratio

EXERCISE 2

Jenny Chang, a sole trader, wishes to assess her business's performance over the last 2 years using the following information.

	Year 1	Year 2
	£000s	£000s
Sales Revenue (net)	220	320
Cost of Sales	120	190
Opening inventory	30	40
Closing inventory	20	30
Gross profit	84	98
Profit for the year	42	70
Opening equity	300	350
Current assets	180	200
Current liabilities	90	80

Calculate the following ratios for both years:

(a) Gross profit %
(b) Profit for the year %
(c) Return on equity employed
(d) Current ratio
(e) Rate of inventory turnover
(f) Expenses ratio

contd

EXERCISE 3

1. Harry Mack is a sole trader and provides you with the following information relating to the last 3 years of his business. You should calculate the return on capital employed ratio for each of the 3 years.
2. State which year had the greatest return on capital employed.

	Year 1	Year 2	Year 3
	£	£	£
Equity at start	120 000	130 000	140 000
Add profit	20 000	30 000	10 000
	140 000	160 000	150 000
Less drawings	10 000	20 000	50 000
Equity at end	130 000	140 000	100 000

ONLINE TEST

Test your knowledge of accounting ratios at www.brightredbooks.net/N5Accounting

ONLINE

For even more practise at accounting ratios head to www.brightredbooks.net/N5Accounting

EXERCISE 4

Dorothy Taylor has provided the following information for her first year in business.

Sales Revenue: £200 000
Gross Profit Percentage: 15%
Profit for the year Percentage: 10%
Return on Equity Employed: 10%

Calculate the following showing all workings:

1. Gross profit
2. Cost of sales
3. Profit for the year
4. Expenses
5. Equity invested

EXERCISE 5

Sean Devine has provided the following information for his first year in business.

Sales Revenue: £150 000
Gross Profit Percentage: 25%
Profit for the year Percentage: 20%
Return on Equity Employed: 5%

Calculate the following showing all workings:

1. Gross profit
2. Cost of sales
3. Profit for the year
4. Expenses
5. Equity invested

SUMMARY

RATIO ANALYSIS

Why use accounting ratios?

- Ratios help with future planning, for example, action can be taken to reduce business expenses to improve profit for the year.
- Ratios can be used to compare one business with another. This can help to highlight why one business may be under-performing.
- Ratios can be used to compare current business performance with previous years.
- Ratios can be used to compare with the industry average and highlight whether one business is performing better or worse than the average firm.
- Ratios can be used to highlight concerns over profitability, liquidity and efficiency.
- Ratios can be used to provide information to encourage potential lenders to lend to or invest in the business.

PROFIT MAXIMISATION AND LIMITING FACTORS

Most sole traders set up in business with a view to making a profit, preferably as high a profit as possible. Maximising profit simply means making as much profit as possible from the resources available. This is usually achieved by making as much as can be sold – if demand for a product is limited, there is no point in making more even though it may be possible to do so.

LIMITING FACTORS

Sometimes demand for a product may be high but production of the product may be limited by factors such as:

- scarcity of materials
- shortage of labour
- limited machine capacity
- limited number of machines
- limited space in a factory.

These factors are called **limiting factors** (or **key factors**). If a limiting factor exists, management will have to decide which level of output will make most profit, taking into account the **limiting factor**. Instead of studying the contribution per unit, contribution must be considered in light of the limiting factor.

EXAMPLE

Two products, A and B are being produced and details are as follows:

	A	B
Contribution per unit (Selling Price – Variable Cost)	£12	£12
Number of labour hours per unit	4 hrs	2 hrs
Number of units demanded	10 000	12 000
Total labour hours available (Limiting Factor)	**60 000 hours**	
Total fixed costs	£160 000	

If demand is to be satisfied the total number of labour hours required would be:

Product A	Product B	
10 000 × 4 +	12 000 × 2	
40 000 +	24 000	= 64 000 hours

The number of labour hours required is **64 000 but only 60 000 labour hours are available**. Since there is a **shortage of 4000, hours**, labour is the limiting factor. How will this problem be solved? Should **one or both products be cut back**? B has a lower **unit contribution** than A so should only B be reduced? Before a decision is taken, the **contribution per labour hour** must be examined.

	A	B
Contribution per unit	£12	£12
Number of labours hours	4 hrs	2 hrs
Contribution per labour hour	**(£12/4 hrs = £3)** £3 per labour hr	**(£12/2 hrs = £6)** £6 per labour hr

Only now can the order of priority be decided. Since the product giving the highest **contribution per labour hour** is B, the full demand for B will be met and the production of A will be cut by 4000 hours. Thus, production will be planned as follows:

1	Product B	24 000 hours/2 hrs		= 12 000 units
2	Product A	60 000 - 24 000 hours	= 36 000 hours/4	= 9000 units

How Much Profit will be Made?

	A	B	Total
Number of labour hours	36 000	24 000	60 000
Contribution per labour hour	£3	£6	
Total contribution	£3 x 36 000	£6 x 24 000	
	£108 000	£144 000	**£252 000**
Less fixed costs			£160 000
Profit (maximised)			**£92 000**

DON'T FORGET

When there is a limiting factor involved - you must find contribution per limiting factor!

contd

EXERCISE 1

John Craig is a sole trader who produces two items, **rugs** and **scarves**. Figures available are as follows:

Total labour hours available	20 000 hours
Total fixed costs	£200 000

NOTE: The limiting factor is 20 000 labour hours.

Product	Rugs	Scarves
Selling price per unit	£80	£20
Variable costs per unit	£40	£8
Contribution per unit (Selling Price – Variable Cost)	?	?
Labour hours per unit	2	1
Number of units demanded	5000	12 000

(a) Compare the hours available with the hours required to find the shortage of labour hours.
(b) What is limiting factor for John Craig?
(c) Calculate the contribution per unit for each product.
(d) Calculate the contribution per labour hour for each product.
(e) Show the order of priority for production. Give a reason for your answer.
(f) Show how many labour hours should be allocated to the production of both rugs and scarves.
(g) Find the total contribution from the rugs and scarves.
(h) Subtract the total fixed costs to find the total profit from the production of both products.

EXERCISE 2

James Wilson is a sole trader who makes three products, X, Y and Z, and has provided the following information:

Total machine hours available	22 000 hours
Total fixed costs	£140 000

NOTE: The limiting factor is 22 000 machine hours

Product	X	Y	Z
Selling price per unit	£26	£48	£568
Variable cost per unit	£16	£32	£40
Contribution per unit (SP-VC)	?	?	?
Number of machine hours per unit	1	2	1.5
Number of units demanded	4000	6000	5000

(a) Compare the hours available with the hours required to find the shortage of machine hours.
(b) What is the limiting factor for James Wilson?
(c) Calculate the contribution per unit for each product.
(d) Calculate the contribution per machine hour for each product.
(e) Show the order of priority for production. Give a reason for your answer.
(f) Show how many machine hours should be allocated to the production of the three products.
(g) Find the total contribution from the production of all three products.
(h) Calculate the maximum possible profit from the production of all three products.

EXERCISE 3

David Main currently manufactures four products, Alpha, Beta, Gamma and Omega.
Annual fixed costs are £131 500
Details for each product are shown below.

	Alpha	Beta	Gamma	Omega
Selling price	£33	£35	£42	£42
Variable costs	£16.50	£21	£18	£22
Contribution per Unit	?	?	?	?
Labour Hours	3	4	4	5

During the next year the number of labour hours is likely to be limited to **46 000 hours**.

Demand for each of the four products is estimated to be:
Alpha – 5000 units
Beta – 4000 units
Gamma – 3000 units
Omega – 3500 units
You are required to:
(a) Calculate the **contribution per unit** for each product.
(i) Calculate the **contribution per labour** hour for each product.
(ii) State the **order of production** to maximise profit.
(b) Calculate the amount of each product to be produced if profits are to be maximised.
(c) Calculate the total contribution per product and overall profit if profits are to be maximised.

contd

PROFIT MAXIMISATION AND LIMITING FACTORS (CONTD)

EXERCISE 4

John Devine is a sole trader who uses general purpose machines which are equally suitable for making any of the company's products. Machining capacity is limited to a maximum of 60000 machine hours per year.

Fixed costs run at £90000.

Maximum sales demand in units is expected to be:

Product K – 5000 units, Product L – 5000 units, Product M – 10000 units

The following information relates to products K, L and M:

PER UNIT	K	L	M
Variable costs	£22	£16	£6
Contribution	£8	£4	£9
Machine hours	4	4	3

You are required to:

(a) Calculate the selling price per unit for each product. (Hint: variable costs + contribution).
(b) Calculate the contribution per machine hour for each product. (Hint: contribution per unit divided by machine hours).
(c) State the order in which the products should be produced. (NOTE – QUANTITIES ARE NOT REQUIRED).
(d) Calculate the quantity of each product that should be produced to maximise total profit, within the existing 60000 machine hour capacity.
(e) Calculate the maximum total profit.
(f) Calculate the reduction in profit shown in your answer to (e) if company policy dictates that at least 3500 units of each product must be produced and sold.

(Hint: Hours should be transferred from the unit that gives the second highest contribution per machine hour and given to the production of the product where production is less than 3500 units)

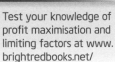

ONLINE TEST

Test your knowledge of profit maximisation and limiting factors at www.brightredbooks.net/N5Accounting

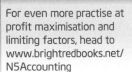

ONLINE

For even more practise at profit maximisation and limiting factors, head to www.brightredbooks.net/N5Accounting

THINGS TO DO AND THINK ABOUT

ASSESSMENT/EXTENSION TASK

Christine Black is a sole trader who currently manufactures four products A, B, C and D.
Annual fixed costs are £300000
Details for each product are shown below.

	A	B	C	D
	£	£	£	£
Selling Price	46	55	62	45
Variable Costs:				
Materials	21	30	22	23
Labour (£2 per hour)	6	8	10	6
Expenses	–	–	2	–
Variable overheads	8.5	6	9	7

During the next year, the number of labour hours is likely to be **limited to 280000 hours**. Demand for each of the four products is estimated to be:

A – 25000 units, B – 20000 units, C – 18000 units, D – 18500 units

You are required to:

(a) Calculate the contribution per unit for each product.
(b) (i) Calculate the **contribution per labour hour** for each product.
    (ii) State the **order of production** to maximise profit.
(c) Calculate the output of each product if profits are to be maximised.
(d) Calculate the total contribution per product and overall profit if profits are to be maximised.

GLOSSARY

Accrual – an expense still owing at the end of an accounting period. It will appear as a current liability in the statement of financial position.

Bank Overdraft – when more money has been taken out of a current account than has been deposited. A bank overdraft is usually organised with a bank in advance and interest is usually charged on amounts overdrawn.

Bin Card – this is a document which sits alongside 'bins' in a store room. Bin cards are updated when inventory is removed. Bin cards aim to ensure accurate inventory records are available for each item of inventory.

Bonus – an additional payment offered as an incentive to employees to try and achieve production/output targets.

Break-even – the level of output at which the business does not make a profit or a loss.

Business Expenses – expenses which are necessary for running a business, e.g. electricity, gas, insurance and telephone.

Capital – money or other assets used to start up a business.

Carriage Inwards – this is like a delivery charge. If our suppliers deliver our purchases to our business, they may charge us for doing so. This makes our purchases more expensive. This must therefore be added to our purchases figure.

Carriage Outwards – this is a business expense. This is when the seller agrees to pay for goods to be delivered to the customer.

Cash Budget – a statement prepared to show inflows and outflows of cash for a business. They can be used to predict periods of potential cash shortages or possible liquidity problems.

Cash Discount – a reduction in the amount due to be paid by the purchaser to the seller for prompt payment. For example, if a customer pays the seller within 30 days they are entitled to a 5% discount.

Cash Receipt – a document used to record payment made by cash.

Cash Register (Till) Receipt – a document used to record cash sales, that is cash received from customers for goods sold.

Cheque – a document that orders the payment of money from one bank account into another – usually a current account.

Cheque Foil – document used to record payment received by cheque.

Cheque Counterfoil – a document used to record payment made by cheque.

Closing Balance – usually refers to cash or inventory. This is the amount of inventory or cash left in the business at the end of an accounting period. Closing inventory will normally become the opening inventory for the next accounting period.

Closing Inventory – this is the unsold inventory that is left at the end of the accounting period. This must be deducted, as it will not be sold until the next accounting period, that is it will become opening inventory in the next accounting period.

Contribution – the difference between selling price and variable costs. Contribution initially goes towards paying fixed costs.

Copy Credit Note – an exact copy of the copy credit note sent to the purchaser. The seller keeps a copy of all credit notes sent as this provides a record of all sales returns.

Copy Invoice – an exact copy of the Invoice sent to the purchaser. The seller keeps a copy of all invoices sent as a record of goods sold.

Cost Centre – an area of responsibility where costs can be charged, for example a department. Each department in your school, for example the English and Maths departments are treated as cost centres.

Cost Unit – the actual product being made, e.g. a pen or a cake.

Credit Note – a document sent by the seller to the purchaser when the purchaser returns goods to the seller because they are faulty or the wrong goods have been dispatched.

Current Assets – these consist of items which are held for a short period of time. Their monetary value will be constantly changing throughout the accounting year. Current assets usually consist of:

Inventory
Trade Receivables
Other Receivables
Bank ⎫
Cash ⎭ Cash and Cash Equivalents

Current Liabilities – these are amounts owing by the business to individuals or other business. Current liabilities usually consist of:

Trade Payables
Small Loans
Accruals
Bank Overdraft

Depreciation – the fall in value of an asset due to wear and tear, age or usage. Annual depreciation appears as an expense in the profit and loss account and aggregate depreciation is shown in the statement of financial position.

Direct Costs – a cost which can be identified directly with the making of a product. For example, wood used to make a desk. You can easily identify the wood in the desk.

Discount Allowed – a cash discount allowed by a firm to its customers when they pay their debts/accounts quickly.

Discount Received – a cash discount received when a firm pays amounts owing quickly.

Double-Entry Bookkeeping – a system used for recording the financial transactions of a business. Every debit entry must have a corresponding credit entry.

Drawings – money taken out of the business by the owner for his/her own personal use. This normally consists of a sum of money each month but could also include items of inventory, if removed from the business for personal use.

Expenses – these are costs which the business must pay if the business is to function properly and may include items such as electricity, telephone and insurance.

FIFO – a system of issuing stock to 'jobs' where the first inventory purchased by the business is the first inventory removed and issued to jobs. The oldest inventory is issued first. The system may be used when inventory is subject to deterioration.

Final Accounts – the term used to describe the final accounts of a business, that is income statement and statement of financial position.

Financial Accounting – the preparation of financial statements such as income statements and statements of financial position.

Fixed Costs – these remain constant and do not change with the level of production. For example rent. Whether you sell 0 units or 100 000 units, rent will remain the same.

Gross Pay – pay earned by an employee prior to the deduction of income tax, national insurance and any other deductions.

Gross Profit – the profit a business makes from buying goods at a certain price and selling them at a higher price. This is the profit before expenses are deducted.

Indirect Costs – these cannot be seen or even traced to the product being made. These are overheads such as rent or heat and light. However, without these costs the product would not be able to have been produced.

Invoice – a document sent to the purchaser by the seller requesting payment when goods are sold on credit. An invoice is similar to a 'bill'.

Job Costing – an accounting system for calculating the cost of completing a job to a customer's specifications and determining the selling price.

Labour Remuneration – methods of financially rewarding labour for services provided. For example, wages may be calculated on a time-based system or on a piece-work system.

Ledger – a book used for storing individual ledger accounts. Many ledgers are now managed electronically using computer software packages.

Ledger Account – an individual account within a ledger. A ledger account records all transactions relating to a particular asset or particular expense.

LIFO – a system of issuing inventory to 'jobs' where the last inventory purchased by the business is the first inventory removed from the stores and issued to jobs. The newest or more recent inventory is issued first.

Limiting Factor – a factor which restricts the output of a business, for example, it could refer to a shortage of skilled labour hours, or a shortage of machine hours.

Liquidity – when a business has enough inflows of money to meet all financial outgoings. Or when current assets are enough to meet current liabilities.

Loan – amounts borrowed by a business. Banks often provide loans to businesses. Loan are repaid over a number of months or years and interest is charged on the amount borrowed.

Management Accounting – this has it focus on providing the management or owner of an organisation with information on costs to enable them to make decisions for the businesses future.

Margin of Safety – difference between the current level of output and the level of output at break-even point. Margin of safety can be expressed in units or sales value.

Mark-up – a percentage added on to the total cost of a job in order to provide a profit.

Maximum Inventory – the maximum amount of inventory a business should hold. Holding too much inventory could lead to a deterioration of inventory and incur high storage costs.

Minimum Inventory – the minimum amount of inventory a business should hold. If sufficient inventory is not held by the business, then the business could run out of inventory which could result in a delay in completing customers' orders.

Net Current Assets – the figure arrived at when current liabilities are subtracted from current assets.

Net Pay – another name for take home pay. It is simply gross pay less all deductions such as income tax and national insurance.

Net Sales – the sales figure less sales returns.

Non-Current Assets – these consist of property of a durable nature, likely to be in the business for a considerable period of time, at least a year. They are usually high in monetary value and consist of things like:
- Property
- Fixtures and Fittings
- Furniture
- Machinery
- Motor Vehicles

Opening Balance – usually refers to cash or inventory. This is the amount of inventory or cash available to a firm at the beginning of an accounting period.

Opening Capital – the amount the sole trader invests at the start of business.

Opening Inventory – inventory left over from last year (last accounting period). We would try to sell this inventory first before any of the inventory newly purchased.

Overhead Absorption – a method of charging a cost centre's overheads to cost units. For example, overheads may be charged to cost units on the basis of direct labour hours or on the basis of direct materials used.

Overhead Allocation – when an overhead can be directly charged to one specific cost centre and therefore no need to apportion or share it between a number of cost centres.

Overhead Apportionment – a method of 'sharing' an overhead expense between a number of cost centres. Over apportionment occurs when an overhead cannot be charged directly to one specific cost centre.

Overtime Payments – amounts paid to employees for working additional hours above their agreed contract hours. Overtime payments are usually paid at a higher rate, e.g. time and half.

Perpetual Inventory System – a stocktaking system whereby the stock balance is shown on the stock record card after every receipt or issue of inventory.

Piece-work Rate System – a method of paying workers based on the units of output produced.

Prepayment – an expense which has been paid in advance at the end of an accounting period. It will appear as a current asset in the statement of financial position.

Prime Cost – this is the total of direct materials, direct labour and other direct expenses used to make a product. Prime cost is basically a term used to describe the initial or first costs of the production process.

Production Budget – a document prepared to forecast future production requirements for a business.

Production Cost Centre – a department or area of a business where costs can be allocated or apportioned to. Production cost centres are directly involved in the making of a product or provision of a service.

Profit and Loss Account – an account prepared (usually annually) which calculates profit of the year. It is prepared by subtracting expenses from gross profit (and any other monies received by the business).

Profit for the Year – the figure arrived at when expenses are deducted from gross profit.

Purchases – this is the term used to describe items purchased which will then be re-sold.

Purchases Returns – these are purchases which have been returned to the supplier, perhaps because they are faulty.

Re-order Level – the level of inventory that should trigger a purchase order to be made. The re-order level will be dependent on factors such as delivery times/dates offered by the supplier.

Re-order Quantity – the amount of inventory that should be requested each time a purchase order is made.

Sales – this is the name given to the value of the goods sold during the trading period. The sales figure is the first figure entered in the trading account.

Sales Budget – a document prepared to forecast future sales of a business.

Sales Returns – sometimes customers will return goods that we have sold them. This may be because they are faulty or we sent them the wrong quantity. Sales returns must be deducted from sales in order to arrive at an accurate sales figure for the accounting period.

Service Cost Centre – a department or area of a business where costs can be allocated or apportioned to. Service cost centres are not directly involved in the making of a product or provision of a service, for example a store's maintenance department.

Sole Trader – a business owned and managed by one person. Sole traders have unlimited liability.

Spreadsheet Software – a general purpose package that is mostly used for carrying out calculations.

Statement of Account – this shows a summary of transactions which have taken place (between a buyer and seller) for a given period of time – usually one month. This allows the buyer to pay for his goods at the end of each month rather than write a cheque for each individual invoice received.

Statement of Financial Position – a STATEMENT which shows the value of the assets, liabilities and capital of a sole trader.

Stock Card – this is similar to a bin card. It is used to record stock movements, that is issues and receipts of stock. However, it will also record the prices of stock issues and receipts. Stock cards can be managed electronically using computer software.

Suspense Account – a temporary account that is used when a trial balance fails to agree. If the debit side of a trial balance totals to £500 and the credit side totals to £600 a suspense account will be created with a debit balance of £100.

Time Based System – a method of paying workers based on the time they work, for example £10 per hour for a 40-hour week.

Total Costs – when fixed costs and variable costs are added together.

Total Sales – this is calculated by multiplying unit selling price by the number of units sold.

Trade Discount – a reduction in the amount due to be paid by the purchaser to the seller. Trade discount is offered to regular customers or to customers who buy in bulk.

Trade Payables – individuals or businesses who we owe money to. They are current liabilities in the statement of financial position.

Trade Receivables – individuals or businesses who owe our business money. They are current assets in the statement of financial position.

Trading Account – an account prepared (usually annually) which calculates gross profit. It shows the difference between net sales and the cost of sales.

Trial Balance – an account prepared to check the accuracy of double-entry bookkeeping. If ledger accounts are accurate then a trial balance will agree.

Turnover – another name used by accountants, for net sales, that is sales less sales returns.

Unlimited Liability – when the owner of a business (sole trader) can be held responsible for the debts of their business and could lose their personal assets, for example their house or car.

Variable Costs – these are costs that change or vary with the number of units being produced, e.g., materials used in production. The more units produced the higher will be the variable cost.

VAT – a tax charged on the supply of most goods and services in the United Kingdom. A business acts as a collector of VAT for the government.